Have Saddle, Will Travel

Have Saddle, Will Travel

Low-Impact Trail Riding and Horse Camping

Don West

STOREY
BOOKS

North Adams, Massachusetts

*The mission of Storey Communications
is to serve our customers
by publishing practical information
that encourages personal independence
in harmony with the environment.*

Edited by Deborah Burns and Ruth Strother
Art direction and cover design by Meredith Maker
Front cover: Top left, top right, and lower right
    photos by Giles Prett; lower left photo courtesy
    of Don West
Text design by Tom Morgan, Blue Design
Text production by Jennifer Jepson Smith
    and Meredith Maker
Photographs by Giles Prett, with the following excep-
    tions: pages v, viii, ix, x, xi, 4, 7, 9, 19, 22, 48, 53, 55,
    56, 60, 61, 62, 63, 64, 68, 69, 70, 72, 80, 81, 82, 97,
    100, 105, 106, 118, 119, 126 courtesy of Don West;
    pages 84, 111, 112, © Curtis Martin; page 6, Photodisc;
    pages 6, 96, 98, and 101, Corbis.
Maps from U. S. Geological Survey, Denver, Colorado
Indexed by Susan Olason/Indexes & Knowledge Maps

Printed in Canada by Transcontinental-Interglobe
10 9 8 7 6 5 4 3 2 1

Library of Congress Cataloging-in-Publication Data

West, Don (Donald Parker)
    Have saddle, will travel: low-impact trail riding and horse camping / by Don West.
        p.   cm.
    "Parts of this book were previously self-published by Don West and titled Have saddle — will travel" - T.p. verso.
    ISBN 1-58017-371-3 (alk. paper)
    1. Low-impact trail riding. 2. Low-impact camping. 3. Packhorse camping. I. Title.

SF309.28 .W47 2001
798.2'3-dc21
2001018

My wife, Maria, and I set off on an afternoon ride.

Born to Ride

I'm a cowboy and
it shows on my face
a spirit of adventure
that time can't erase

I'm a cowboy
and my word is my deed
I'm traveling light
on the back of my steed

I'm a cowboy
it's a feeling inside
I drift with the wind
and I float on the tide

I'm a cowboy
and I live wild and free
wherever I end up
that's OK with me

I'm a cowboy
and it can't be denied . . .
'cause I know in my heart
I was born to ride!

— Don West

This book is dedicated to the memory
of my father and my grandfather,
who lit the spark that became a flame,
showing me the way;
the love and inspiration of my wife,
who gave me a reason to care
and a desire to share;
and the hope for my children,
who make me want to do something
to preserve the wild places,
so that they too may have their turn to
experience the adventure.

Contents

Prologue

My grandfather's favorite photograph of himself as a soldier in the United States Cavalry.

As a young boy growing up in eastern Pennsylvania, I used to play by myself in my grandparents' big, dark attic on rainy, gloomy Saturday mornings. There were many long-forgotten treasures carefully stored away in that special place, relics of a past period, a more romantic and slow-moving time, forever lost, never to come again.

Among the dusty cardboard boxes, steamer trunks, and wooden sea captain's chests was a big, handsome, dapple-gray rocking horse. Hung in an antique stand-up cedar closet, scented with mothballs, was a well-worn wool army uniform, the type worn by Teddy Roosevelt's Rough Riders. Thrown into a corner was a beat-up old McClellan saddle. On the floor, in front of a tall dressing mirror, was a pair of shiny brown riding boots. And hung unceremoniously from a nail by its chin strap was a faded, flat-brimmed campaign hat.

Shut away behind the door of this dingy, musty sanctuary were all the ingredients necessary to stir a young boy's fertile imagination and fill a few dreary hours with unfettered flights of fantasy. Dressed in that old uniform jacket, wearing the hat and boots, and riding the rocking horse in front of the mirror, I entered a private world of my own creation. Those forsaken treasures were the springboard to a fantasy world, where a man on a horse was the master of his own destiny, a real-life hero.

My grandfather came to Pennsylvania from England as a teenager, just after the turn of the century. When he turned eighteen he joined the United States Army. He was loaded into a troop train and sent out west to El Paso, Texas, where he was stationed in the Cavalry — the Mounted Engineers. Soon after my grandfather completed boot camp, he and my grandmother were married. They lived in a tent city and rode their horses across the open, rolling border country along the Rio Grande.

As far back as I can remember, my grandfather loved to tell stories about his days in the army. His favorites were always the ones about his daring days on horseback. I came to realize that those romanticized tales were built upon the memories of the happiest times of his life. His favorite photograph of himself showed a handsome young man astride a big, rawboned army remount horse. He cut quite a dashing figure, outfitted in the same hat, uniform, and riding boots I had found tucked away in the attic.

I will never forget the look on my grandfather's face when, in his late eighties, he visited my ranch in western Colorado and saw my Peruvian Paso horses. Although he was getting feeble, a light still burned in his eyes. He told army stories to his grandkids as he bounced them on his knees. Even during his last lonely battles with the ravages of old age, he kept that one special picture of himself propped up on his dresser where he could see it from his bed. He'd sit staring at it for hours, traveling far away in his mind as he relived his private, most vivid, most treasured memories. Visiting him in the little room that had become his final world stirred memories for me, too!

While I was a kid, on occasional Saturdays my father would take me riding at a local Western stable. It was our father-and-son time — just the two of us, doing something special together. It was obvious to me how much my dad enjoyed riding the horses. We used to get out on the trail and race those old nags against each other, riding hell-bent for leather. I don't think he had any idea what those shared moments meant to me or how they would help shape my life.

Much later, when I had children of my own, he and my mother came out to Colorado for a visit. I was working that summer as a cowboy out on a ranch near the town of Crested Butte. For three or four days, Dad rode with me, just the two of us moving cattle across wild and rugged mountain country, packing salt, and doctoring sick cows and calves. It was hard work and required some rough riding, but together we got the job done. Not much was said, but I felt closer to Dad than I had at any other time in my life.

My father died unexpectedly a few years later. At the funeral, my mother said that Dad had told her that cowboying with me was one of the most fun and exciting things he had ever done in his entire life! He had confessed to her that he had been worried that he might not be able to keep up. He was proud that he had been able to ride and do his part. Of course, I hadn't even given it a thought. Even though we were both much older, I was still living with my childhood vision of my father. I never questioned his ability. After all, he was my dad!

Although they never pushed it on me, my father and my grandfather somehow instilled in me a love of freedom and adventure, symbolized by a man on his horse. This image captivated my imagination and made an indelible impression on my young mind. Without realizing it, I had been hooked on horses. My life's dance was already being choreographed to the rhythm of a horse's hoofbeats. This reality, however, became revealed to me only much later. Let me tell you how it happened.

My father and my grandfather gave me a love of freedom and adventure, symbolized by the image of a man on his horse.

I'll never forget my first summer in Colorado, which changed my life and shaped my destiny.

High on a steep, nearly inaccessible rocky ridge in the heart of the Elk Mountains of Colorado, where Snowmass Mountain joins the Maroon Bells at a lonely outpost far above timberline, a tiny saddle with a small sign reads "Trail Riders Pass." On one side of the trail, Snowmass Lake nestles in a basin thousands of feet below, carved out more than ten thousand years ago by receding glaciers. On the opposite side lies Geneva Lake and below that lies Lead King Basin. A tiny thread of a trail winds its way through the mountains, joining these two beautiful, remote wilderness areas. It was along this little-traveled trail in the summer of 1964 — my first summer in Colorado — that I had an encounter with destiny that I will never forget. As brief as it was, it left a permanent image in my mind's eye and influenced the course of my life.

I was in my early twenties. I was a mountaineering instructor, shepherding a group of teenage Outward Bound students up a rugged mountain trail. The night before we had camped at Geneva Lake. It's a breathtakingly beautiful spot, just below timberline, set against the perfect backdrop of the S-ridge of Snowmass Mountain, one of Colorado's most magnificent 14,000-foot peaks. As was the custom, we had chopped a hole in the ice that still covered the lake and jumped in, one at a time. We called this moment of madness our early morning dip. Shivering and frozen half to death, we quickly pulled on our clothes, shouldered our packs, and hit the trail just to warm up.

The day had dawned with a brilliant red sky to the east, reminding me of my grandfather's saying, "Red sky in morning, sailors take warning; red sky at night, sailors delight." Just as might be expected, the weather soon deteriorated into a cloudy drizzle. Although the temperature wasn't much above freezing, we soon became sweaty and uncomfortable under our foul-weather gear and heavy packs. The chill of the morning dip was quickly forgotten, replaced by the reality of the task at hand. Even so, I kept a close eye on my students. This was hypothermia weather. Now and then the clouds lifted just enough for me to see the trail up ahead. It switched back and forth, making its way steadily upward toward the little saddle in the skyline ridge, somewhere far above. As we got closer, I thought I saw a figure — a silhouette on the pass that hadn't been there before. Suddenly, the clouds rolled back in. The ghostlike form was gone. A few moments later, there it was again. I could just make out the statuesque figure of a man . . . on a horse!

A surge of excitement went through me. My curiosity was piqued. I wanted to meet this lone stranger on horseback, out here in the middle of nowhere. Even at this distance, something about him seemed very familiar, like an old, long-forgotten friend. I had a strong sense of déjà-vu. The entire scene had a dreamlike quality. I nearly pinched myself to see if I was really awake.

Sitting quietly on his horse, the man waited for us to reach the top of the pass. As my patrol struggled wearily over the crest, I realized that this lone horseman reminded me of that old picture of my grandfather. He was an older man, probably in his early fifties, wearing a campaign hat and riding a McClellan saddle just like my grandfather's. His bedroll was tied on behind him above two large, oversize saddlebags. At his hip he carried a pistol. He cut quite a romantic pose, sitting so relaxed and confident on his dark bay horse as the clouds blew in and out around us, adding to the surrealistic effect.

I don't remember our conversation. We exchanged only a few words, but I felt a strong, almost spiritual connection with this man. It was as though we shared some common bond — a man-to-man understanding of our places in the universe — unspoken, yet acknowledged. Just being in his presence was exciting. After a few moments, we ended our polite exchange and nodded our heads, and he headed on down the trail, the way we had come. With my patrol, I crossed over the ridge and started the long, slow decent toward Snowmass Lake. In a moment the horseman disappeared from sight, but the image of that lone rider on Trail Riders Pass stuck in my memory. The idea of traveling on horseback haunted my thoughts.

I couldn't help feeling as though I had received some kind of sign, as though someone had shown me a locked, secret door and handed me the key. Soon after, I bought a horse and started to make solo trips into the backcountry. Thus began my journey from fantasy to reality, playing the game I have come to call low-impact horse camping.

More than thirty years have passed since that chance encounter on Trail Riders Pass. My grandfather and father have both passed on to their final adventures. Still, I carry their memory and their spirit with me as I continue my horseback trips into the backcountry. For me, the desire to see what lies over that next ridge is as strong as ever. It is the call to raw adventure, a covenant passed on by those self-reliant heroes who went before. I will follow their example, ride in their hoof-prints, and dog their trail for as long as I can. I invite you to pack your gear, saddle your horse, and come along. Take the challenge. Join in the adventure! Saddle up and let's ride! Who knows what you might discover! 🐎

CHAPTER ONE

Simplest
Is Best

CREATING MY OWN REALITY

n my Boy Scout field book there was a full-page picture of a smiling, clean, neat, fresh-as-a-pin, lily-white boy, dressed in an official Boy Scout uniform. He was fully equipped with all kinds of official Boy Scout paraphernalia. He looked as if he could step right off the page and go hiking and camping. Even now, in my mind's eye, I can still see him. He looked so proud, so confident, so self-assured, ready to stride down the trail and tackle any of life's challenges head-on. He was obviously living the Scout motto: Be prepared. I studied that picture carefully. Here was an official role model I could follow, a hero from among my peers. Yes! I wanted to be a Scout just like him!

All winter long, our Scout troop had planned for our annual spring "Camparee." When the long-awaited Saturday morning finally arrived, we lined up outside the community center on the manicured green grass, under a brilliant blue sky, each of us looking as "official" as the smiling boy in the book's picture. At last, our time was at hand. We, too, were going hiking and camping!

Of course, we were all dressed in our official Scout uniforms. We looked sharp in the quasi–military-style shirts and shorts, bedecked with brightly colored badges, pins, and insignia. Around our necks were tied the traditional neckerchiefs that identify Scouts around the world. On our heads we wore the snappy fore-and-

The simplest way is usually the best way.

This photo in my Boy Scout manual was my first inspiration. The photo opposite shows how I travel today.

aft caps made popular by our troops in World War II. But that wasn't all. To really be official you needed Scout shoes: sturdy lace-up Buster Browns, with an imitation moccasin toe. They were indestructible, even if not flexible.

Then there was all that official hiking equipment. On one side of my belt hung my Scout knife and a coil of rope that looked like clothesline, with a snap on one end and a ring on the other. (Come to think of it, I never did figure out exactly what that was for.) On the other hip I wore a hatchet and a hunting knife, in a combination leather sheath. On my back was my official Boy Scout haversack, a sort of canvas pillowcase with shoulder straps, embossed with the official Scout insignia. It was stuffed full to overflowing with all the things my mother and father thought I would need for an overnight camping trip, including my pillow and pajamas.

Shoulder to shoulder, we lined up for inspection. After pledging allegiance to the flag and reciting the Boy Scout Oath and Scout Laws out loud, it was finally time to start hiking! Each patrol carried maps that laid out our route: along back streets, through blue-collar neighborhoods of small brick homes and tiny yards, toward the county park. We marched along, block after block, on uneven concrete sidewalks, cracked and heaved up by overgrown sycamore roots. Our leaders followed at a discreet distance, in their cars, of course, there to give encouragement or lend assistance to the weary, whining, or wounded.

One kid carried our troop flag on a long pole. He was called the "guide-on." The rest of us dutifully followed behind. The day got hotter. It didn't take long before the heavy hatchet began to pull me off balance. The handle created an annoying counter-cadence, beating against my hipbone and thigh. With every step the pocketknife swung up in an arch and tried to slap me in the groin. Every now and then it succeeded. The coiled rope, so neat and official looking during inspection, worked its way loose and began to unravel, threatening to trip me. Its big metal snap rhythmically whacked me in the knee. The pack got heavier, minute by minute. The flimsy canvas straps rolled up like skinny ropes and ate into my shoulder blades. Within fifteen minutes, and with five miles of monotonous, nondescript suburbia left to go, I wondered what fiend had thought up this form of torture.

There is no teacher like experience when it comes to figuring out the best way to do things. It's hard to learn from mistakes you've never made.

I survived my first Camparee and went on to become the first Eagle Scout in my town, one of my proudest accomplishments.

From the comfort of their cars, watching us trudge along, our proud Scout leaders smiled approvingly at us. They must have thought, Look at them! Aren't they having fun! (And adults wonder why there is a generation gap!) So much for adult-child communication.

By the time we crossed under the park gateway, it was mid-afternoon. My Buster Browns had eaten silver-dollar-sized holes in the back of my socks. Bright red blisters had filled the void. My pack felt like it had cut deep trenches into my shoulders. The ax handle had given me a big purple bone bruise that throbbed in time with every step.

As I looked around at the glazed eyes and exhausted faces of my companions, I could see that I had fared no worse than the others. In fact, quite a few had given up, accepting the humiliation of riding with the dads, rather than suffering with those of us who chose to hang tough and stick with the hiking.

Under the shade of the ancient oaks, spread like a lofty canopy over the park's rolling lawns and scattered picnic tables, I threw myself full length on my back and closed my eyes. In a relieved stupor, I lay there, contemplating my misery. I analyzed the myth created by the picture of the clean young Scout, and all that it had conjured up, versus the reality of my present, rather pathetic condition. I asked myself, What's not right with this picture? I realized that if I was going to continue hiking and camping, I would have to reevaluate things, make a few adjustments, and create my own reality. From that point on, my philosophy became "less is best" and "when in doubt, leave it out."

The rest of the Camparee went pretty much as you might expect. The old army pup tents, set up in neat rows on the open lawn, leaked like sieves in a midnight downpour. The trenches we hastily dug around them (as prescribed by our Scout manual, to keep water from running under the tent flaps) weren't appreciated by the park ranger when he showed up the next morning. Neither were the camp chairs and tables that we had laboriously lashed together, using "native materials" chopped down in the park woods. (After all, we had to have something to do with those hatchets and hunting knives, having lugged them so far.) Much to our surprise, the park officials had intended that the firewood we gathered and the rocks we built fireplaces out of should remain part of the natural landscape. Afternoon games had included knife-and-ax-throwing contests and, for some, carving our initials into the giant beech trees scattered here and there throughout the park. Our unbounded, industrious energy had gone awry. In short, enthusiastic and naive, unguided and unsupervised, we were an environmental disaster.

The next morning found us dead tired, soaking wet, covered with mud, and scratching the burning bites from red ants. After reveille, a bedraggled and filthy bunch of kids dutifully lined up once again to pledge allegiance to the flag and take the Scout oaths. This time, some of the oaths definitely weren't official! When it was over, we threw all the wet, filthy gear unceremoniously into the car trunks, and headed for home. At the following week's troop meeting, everyone (once again looking scrubbed and clean) said they had had a great time and wanted to do it again. (This was my first encounter with mass insanity.)

What did I learn from this experience? I learned that pain and suffering are soon forgotten but the sweet pleasure of fulfilled fantasies lingers on and on. I also learned that, in spite of early fiascoes (learning experiences), I liked the outdoors, hiking, and camping. I realized that there is no teacher like experience when it comes to figuring out the best way to do things. It's hard to learn from mistakes you've never made. Knowledge acquired through books is no substitute for what you learn through the seat of your pants. But a book may ignite your imagination and spur you to action. It may also save you from unnecessary pitfalls.

Way back then, I learned an important lesson: *The simplest way is usually the best way.* It wasn't until I was a sophomore in college, studying American literature, that I became acquainted with the writings of a kindred spirit, Henry David Thoreau. Even to a young Scout on a Camparee, Thoreau's poignant phrase, "simplify, simplify, simplify," would have made good sense. That philosophy became one of my basic guiding principles for what eventually developed into a lifelong pursuit, a game that I created for myself. It's a game that I choose to play by some self-imposed rules in order to give my activities parameters and my life meaning. I call it low-impact horse camping. The goal isn't to fight and conquer nature or to flee in fear; it is to flow into understanding. To go right, you must go light, leaving no trace of your passage. Over the course of many years (and many miles), I've learned my lessons in the school of hard knocks. 🐎

GO RIGHT — GO LIGHT

The purpose of low-impact trail riding is to have more fun with less fuss, while causing as little damage to the environment as possible. Pack light so you can keep the number of horses to a minimum. When you pack light, you often can get by without a packhorse, so the trails are minimally affected. In camp, fewer horses means less compaction of the soil, which prohibits plant growth.

Low-impact trail riding means adapting to the rhythm of nature. It means more comfort and less stress for you and your horse. When you are not overburdened with unnecessary equipment or supplies, both you and your horse are free to enjoy the fresh air, the scenery, and the sounds of nature.

Low-impact trail riding means treating the environment with reverence. Don't camp in scenic or high-use areas. Do tie your horses so trees don't get damaged. And always thoroughly clean up after yourself.

Low-impact trail riding brings peace of mind. You know that having enjoyed your adventure, you are leaving the area the way you found it so others can enjoy it too. You know you're doing your part to preserve the environment for generations to come.

LOW-IMPACT HORSE CAMPING

The happiness I experience while traveling through the wilderness on horseback is not the result of my conquering the environment. It comes from temporarily reducing my needs, simplifying my life, determining what is really essential, and being able to get along with just the things I choose to carry.

Just as backpacking gear has evolved from (top) knapsacks and bedrolls to (bottom) lightweight packs and sleeping bags, so have wilderness use policies and practices changed during the last thirty years.

The ability to live for the moment, be self-reliant and flexible, and coexist within the framework of what many consider a hostile environment is what nourishes my spirit.

Going Light

I think of myself as a wandering *conquistador* (Spanish for conqueror) not of the natural world that surrounds me but of the human-made anxiety that exists deep within my inner realm. As my self-selected wilderness adventure unfolds, I find my way deeper into the core of my own being. I become more centered, in tune with the natural rhythm of the universe. Life takes on a new and deeper meaning. Not me against the elements, but me as part of the universe. Taking a horse and going for an extended ride into the backcountry, I choose to go light. In the process, I learn what I can do without.

My avocation as a horseman paralleled my vocation as a mountaineer and backpacker. Fate being what it is, I ended up spending a fair amount of my adult life lugging heavy loads up steep mountain trails; teaching mountaineering, climbing, and backcountry skiing; and living for extended periods of time in the high country. I perfected those skills to a level in which I am able to travel almost anywhere under my own steam for long periods of time, leaving no trace of my passage.

In my lifetime, I have seen backpacking equipment evolve and change dramatically, from crude wooden pack boards and wool blanket bedrolls to sophisticated internal frame packs and lightweight sleeping bags that make a heavy load feel (almost) as light as a feather. During the same period I have seen wilderness use practices (and ethics) change to meet the ever-growing population pressure and to fulfil our desire to experience the wilderness on its own terms — with the least impact.

Horse Packing

Over the years, my interest in traveling and camping on

horseback gained momentum. In my spare time, I began to look for, and experiment with, the few items of packing equipment available to today's horse packer. I read what few books I could find on the subject. Compared to the things backpackers were doing (or not doing), many of the techniques described by horse packers seemed to be about twenty years out of date. The truth is, most of the horse-packing equipment on the market even today looks like it came straight out of an 1890s museum. I guess it's not surprising that many of the attitudes and practices related to traveling and camping in the backcountry, prevalent among dyed-in-the-wool horse packers, match their outdated equipment. When behavior is tied to image, old ideas die hard.

On my first attempt at horse camping, I experimented with the conventional packhorse, packsaddle, and panniers combination. It didn't take long for me to figure out that packing the old-fashioned way wasn't all that much fun. In fact, it was darn hard work! My many years of backpacking experience had already taught me that I could travel light, still be comfortable, and get along just fine. Why did I need to carry the Hilton into the wilderness just because I

My mission was to bring backpacking technology to horse-packing gear, stressing light weight, balance, and compressibility.

wanted to ride my horse? And why be tied down by having to lead another horse around, a constant distraction from enjoying the country I was out there to see? On top of all that, an extra horse literally doubled my impact on the fragile wilderness environment. I decided I'd have to learn how to carry all my necessities with me on my riding horse, just like I saw the stranger doing on Trail Riders Pass.

Selecting and laying out the proper gear was no problem. Packing it so that my horse could carry it comfortably was something else! The only horse pack on the market at that time was an odd-shaped, one-piece duffel bag with multiple zippered compartments. It was slightly contoured to fit behind the cantle of my saddle.

Packing it at home, in the comfort of my living room, wasn't so bad. Trying to pack it out on the trail, especially in a storm, was a nightmare. And my horse wasn't too pleased about having this big floppy thing swung up on him, either. As if that wasn't bad enough, as I used up my food or pulled out and wore the clothing that had provided filler, the remaining gear started to swim around, shifting to the bag's lower ends. It was always trying to pull my saddle off balance, hanging down on one side or the other. In short, it looked good but it didn't work worth a darn.

A Career Change

I realized that if I was going to enjoy this new sport, I'd have to design and make my own packing equipment. I set out to bring to horse-packing gear some of the technology I had seen applied to backpacks. I designed a modular system that allowed me to pack my bags individually. I added compression straps to the bags to tighten down the load. Next, I designed a suspension system to go behind my saddle and hold it all in place. *Voilà!* Saddle Software Systems (SSS) was born. As I tested and refined the SSS saddlebags and packs, other backcountry riders saw and admired my gear. They wanted to know where I got my outfit. Naturally, I told them!

As my various horse-oriented activities began to dominate a larger and larger portion of my life, a career change became inevitable. Having been a backyard breeder of Appaloosas for some ten years, my goal was to have my own horse ranch and become a professional breeder and trainer. I started to look around for a new breed, one that would command a higher price in the equine marketplace. As crazy as it may sound, I wanted to try to make my living with horses and let my other outdoor pursuits become my recreation. After a long com-

parative process, I finally settled on Peruvian Pasos, the world's smoothest riding luxury pleasure horse.

That was more than twenty years ago. I've now owned and trained hundreds of these wonderful horses and established my credentials as a breeder, trainer, teacher, and promoter of naturally gaited, easy riding horses.

I also designed and manufactured a line of saddles and tack specifically suited to the equitation of Paso and other naturally gaited horses. Believing that a happy horse makes for a happy rider, I increased the comfort for the horse by shortening the bar length and adding more rock and flair to the saddletree. Next I designed a wide, flat seat with

---

TRAIL HORSES

I use Peruvian Paso horses on many of my backcountry excursions because I have them, not because they are my number one choice for that type of activity. I chose Peruvian Pasos to breed, raise, and train for the price I thought they could command, not because I believed they were the perfect mountain horse. In fact, Peruvian Paso horses are plantation (flatland) horses, not mountain horses. They are "beautiful to behold, smooth to ride, and easy to handle," a phrase I penned to describe horses and my breeding program when I owned Needle Rock Horse Ranch many years ago. Peruvian Pasos are wonderful

My Paso Pleasure colt, Star.

horses, naturally gaited *(pisos)* and full of manageable energy *(brio)*. They are a luxury pleasure horse, the Rolls Royce of riding horses.

When you think of going into the mountains, however, you don't want a luxury car; you want a Jeep. For mountain riding — especially for overnight trips where the horse is carrying the rider, his saddle and tack, and the gear as well — I would choose a slightly larger, heavier-boned breed, with a little more muscle and a little less nervous energy. American gaited horse breeds, such as Rocky Mountain Horses, Mountain Pleasure Horses, Kentucky Mountain Saddle Horses, Missouri Fox Trotters, and Tennessee Walkers come closer to the type I would choose for the more physically demanding activity of trail riding in the mountains.

We are currently outcrossing our beautiful Peruvian Paso mares with stallions of these breeds to produce a horse we believe will be ideal for our intended use. We call them Paso Pleasure Horses.

Opposite: Misty displays the noble pride and energy that are typical of the Peruvian Paso.

forward-hung stirrups for the rider's comfort and security. My saddles maintain the traditional Spanish or Western look but use American materials and technology. It is a great combination, for both horse and rider. To market these saddles, I traveled around the United States attending horse shows, and thus came up with the company's name, Have Saddle — Will Travel.

A COMFORTABLE HORSE MAKES A HAPPY RIDER

My philosophy is that a comfortable horse is a happy horse, and a happy horse makes a happy rider. The typical Western saddle found in the equine marketplace today is usually built on a tree with bars that are too long and too straight without enough flair at the ends. They often bridge on the horse's back, creating pressure points and sore spots on the horse's shoulder and loins. These saddles were designed for arena roping and riding, not for pleasure trail riding. This is a case of fashion leading function. The end result is that horses ridden over the trails in these saddles are often uncontrollable and unhappy. A good-fitting, comfortable saddle, one designed for riding rough country, is essential for the health and happiness of both horse and rider.

Comfortable Clothing

With packs and saddles out of the way, I began creating comfortable clothing. I liked the looks of traditional Western horseman's garments but needed the comfort, versatility, light weight, and storage capacity of the clothing I'd come to appreciate and enjoy while skiing and mountaineering. I decided to apply the latest high-tech fabrics to classic Western designs, and the Storm Riders line of clothes became reality.

A new business is always an exciting (and high-risk) adventure. Sometimes, when the timing is just right, everything falls into place for a perfect fit. This seems to be such a time.

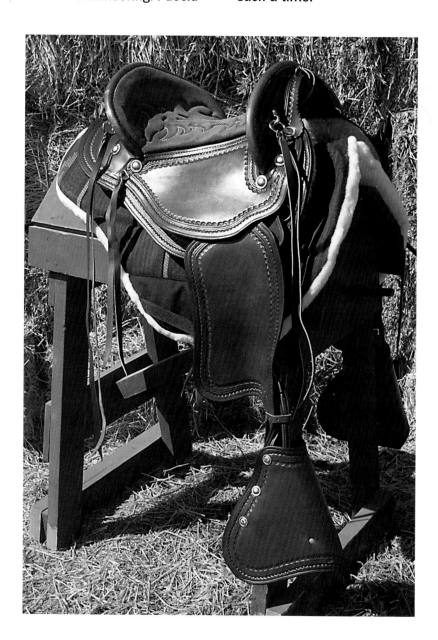

The ideal saddle for trail riding has a wide, flat seat and is comfortable for both horse and rider.

My Pony, My Friend

When all else fails me
When I'm down
in the dumps
When I've taken
my share of Life's lumps
and its bumps

I turn to an old friend
Who won't let me down
Who carries my burdens
With nary a frown

Yes, I saddle my pony
And I head down
the trail
With clear skies
above me
Kickin' dust on my tail

For an hour or two
I leave my troubles behind
I drink in the scenery
Enjoying pure
peace of mind

Caught up in
the moment
We go mile after mile
My frown falls away
And I put on a smile

'Till I'm ready to
come back
And try once again
Still rocked by the rhythm
Of my pony, my friend

— Don West

Leave Nothing but Hoofprints

With the summer's work wrapped up, I was looking forward to having a few days alone in the mountains: just me; my dogs, Nicky and Charlie; and my Peruvian Paso gelding, Caluroso. I had hoped to get away earlier, back in late September, when the aspen leaves were at the height of their color. But a steady flow of customers had postponed my departure. It was already well into October, and only a few days remained before the hunting season brought its annual "orange army" invasion to these otherwise quiet mountains.

As I pulled my pickup truck and trailer into the parking area at the trailhead, I was surprised but pleased to find that I had the place all to myself. I had planned this solo trip as a grand finale to a busy summer spent working with clients. Now it was my time to relax and unwind.

The ride I had mapped out for myself back in the comfort of my living room took me up the Dark Canyon trail and into the Ruby and Ragged Mountain Ranges. This is some of the most remote and rugged country Colorado has to offer. The scenery is world-class, picture-postcard stuff, with fantastic photo opportunities waiting around every corner.

It had been about fifteen years since I had last ridden this trail. In the interim, the Forest Service had developed the trailhead, clearing out numerous parking and camping places for horse packers and hunters. Permanent tie-ups and feed racks had been installed. There were even fancy, brand-new his-and-hers outhouses. Where the trail left the parking area, an information board told riders and hikers that a wilderness area lay ahead. Proper precautions as well as low-impact camping practices were required. The details were well outlined on a Forest Service flyer.

By this point, it was early afternoon. The day had turned gray. Clouds pulled together into a solid dreary ceiling overhead. The temperature dropped to below freezing, and snow flurries sparkled in the air. The snowflakes were so fine, almost invisible, that they reminded me of gossamer ghosts. You could feel them, but they disappeared when you looked straight at them. As I spread out my gear, the sound of silence and my sense of solitude intensified. A shiver ran through my body. I pulled on another layer of clothing and went on packing.

My gear was well-made, lightweight, bare-bones stuff — the same items I would take if I were going backpacking. Everything fit into my two large saddlebags and a contoured cantle bag that tied on behind my saddle. Up front across the

Above: Even in the Rocky Mountains you can find open, fairly level areas that are ideal for pitching camp. Opposite: My faithful companion Nicky leads the way as we explore the Ruby and Ragged Mountain Ranges.

fork of my saddle sat my roomy pommel bags. As I sorted my equipment into separate piles to be packed into the various bags, I went over a mental list of things that I would need. I made sure that I didn't pack too much — or leave anything important out. Finally I was packed and ready.

We ambled along on relatively flat ground for a ways under a canopy of towering old-growth ponderosa pines. The only noise came from the occasional squirrel abandoning his nut-catching duties long enough to scold us for entering his private domain.

Suddenly the trail took a sharp bend to the left. We were faced with our first obstacle: a very narrow bridge made just for horse travel, arching high over Anthracite Creek. The water level was low enough at this time of year that the bridge wasn't really necessary. It was clear, however, from the height of the watermarks on the steep banks that this creek was a rushing torrent during spring and early summer. Although Caluroso had never seen a bridge like this before, he stepped up and crossed it without a moment's hesitation. I was proud of my Paso horse. He was brave and willing. Now I was thoroughly enjoying my solitude!

Looking upstream, I saw the towering cliffs that form the natural stone gateway into the Dark Canyon. The cliff walls gaped like some huge mouth waiting to swallow any unwary traveler. The canyon was so narrow with walls so high and steep that it looked like a giant's cleaver had hacked it with a single stroke. It was hard to believe that there could be room for the trail, let alone the creek, in this narrow gash. I took one long last look, then plunged back into the thicket of dogwoods and alder. My attention was once again focused on the obstacle course underfoot.

For the first few miles, the trail hugged a narrow, flat strip of land between the creek, which had become a roaring set of rapids, and the cliffs towering overhead. In sections where the cliff went right down into the water, the trail climbed steeply in little switchbacks to find a passage between huge boulders and across steep scree slopes. There were unnervingly narrow sections crossing open avalanche chutes, where winter snows came down from open bowls above. One false step here would have meant a sure plunge of hundreds of feet into the roaring creek below. I literally held my breath as Caluroso forged over these dangerous places without a moment's hesitation. If he had panicked or tried to stop and turn around, it would have surely resulted in the death of him or me or both of us. This was not a place for the weak of heart. Nicky and Charlie, totally unaware of my apprehension, cruised on up the trail acting as my scouts.

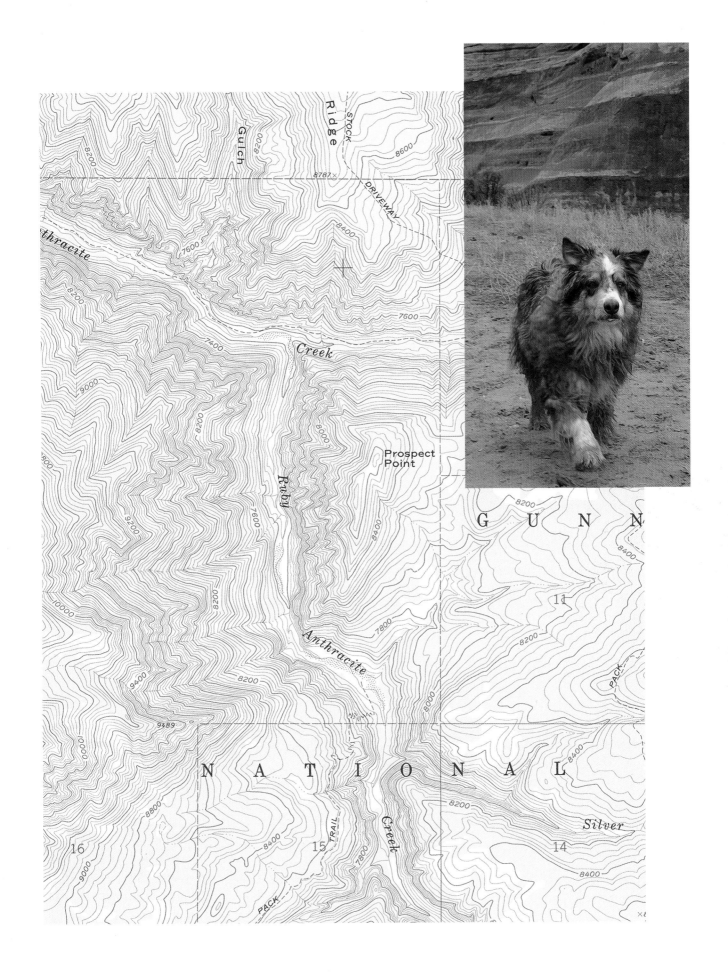

The peaks glistened with fresh snow, white and clear. My water bottles had frozen solid.

Finally we came to a high vantage point. Hundreds of feet below, I could see two streams coming together across the canyon; I looked into the extremely narrow chasm of Ruby Anthracite Creek. Its cascades and pools were locked in place by towering walls, only a stone's throw apart. I reached down and patted Cal's neck, reassuring him and myself.

Another hour brought the four of us to the junction of North Anthracite and Middle Anthracite Creeks. Here the canyon widened out at the foot of a trail that switchbacked up the wall, appropriately called the Devil's Stairway. I decided to make camp there. With only an hour of daylight left, my timing couldn't have been better. I unpacked my gear and unsaddled my horse in a small clearing about a hundred yards from the creek's edge. I hobbled Caluroso in the small meadow. There was plenty of grass. He began munching happily. Within minutes I had my tent up, my air mattress inflated, and my sleeping bag unpacked and fluffed out. Soon, my stove was fired up and a pot of water set to boil for dinner's first course: hot soup!

Right before I crawled into my tent, I attached Caluroso to his high line with a locking aluminum carabiner (an oval ring with a hinged sidegate, often used by mountain climbers) through a figure eight knot at the end of his lead line. Then I snapped the carabiner over a fifty-foot rope stretched overhead between two trees. The high line was attached to the trees with tree-saver straps. An eight-inch-long stick tied in each end of the overhead rope about five feet from each tree kept him from wrapping his lead line around the trees. Now he would be able to continue grazing, and move around a bit during the night without getting himself tangled up. With Nicky and Charlie contentedly curled up beside me in the tent, I fell asleep, warm, dry, and cozy. This was literally a two-dog night!

DAYLIGHT DIDN'T BRING its hoped-for warmth. In the east, at the valley's far end, the Ruby Range towered above the surrounding landscape and sheltered my camp from the sun's rays. The peaks glistened with fresh snow, white and clear. My thermometer read 20°F. My water bottles confirmed the reading. They had frozen solid during the night. Only the call of nature and the need for a fresh, hot cup of coffee prodded me from my tent to greet the new day. An inch or two of fresh snow lay on the ground, but it was as light as a feather. In a few hours, a little sun would quickly melt it and dry things out.

HORSES' FEARS

When horses are frightened by something, their response is to flee. Once they turn their backs on the bogeyman they will run like hell and look back only when they have arrived in safe territory. If they think they are in danger, they want to do this even if people are on their backs. However, the more you make it clear to your horse that you are "top dog" in the pecking order, the more your horse will look to you and ask, "Should I be afraid?"

Until you establish this dominant relationship you must prepare to point your horse toward the object of his fear and let him figure out that it isn't going to hurt him. Trying to do this under precarious trail conditions can be daunting. It is important to establish a relationship with your horse where you are the brains and he is the brawn, but you should do this at home, over time, before you traverse any treacherous trails.

When I first moved to the mountains of Colorado in the mid-1960s, there was so much wild, pristine country, and so few people using it, that I always cooked on an open fire. The only time I used a backpacking stove was when I camped above timberline. In fact, my skills as a backcountry fire maker and accomplished campfire cook were something that I was most proud of. However, things have changed, dramatically. Overuse, especially from campfires and firewood gathering, is evident in every beautiful spot accessible by foot or hoof. To preserve the feeling of unspoiled wilderness, allowing others to have the same "first time" feel that I had, I gave up fires twenty years ago and started cooking on stoves. Given the ever-increasing demand on wild country by city folks seeking recreation, campfires should be taboo in most wilderness country.

One of the first laws of low-impact horse camping is that any trash generated at a wilderness campsite must be carried out and safely disposed of back home.

As I savored my first cup of coffee, I walked around my campsite, conjuring up old memories and trying to stay warm. Near the creek, I found the remains of what appeared to be a hunter's camp left over from the year before. The hunters had left large poles, typically used as skinning and hanging racks for big game, nailed between two trees. There was a worn-out set of hobbles on the ground and some pack cloth nailed to a big tree. They had also left three huge fire rings. Half a dozen short, stout logs, cut from a living tree with a chainsaw (which was illegal in this wilderness area), had apparently been used as campstools. As I looked closer, I saw that the trash had been dumped into a shallow pit and buried. Some critter, probably a skunk or a coyote, had dug it up and scattered cans and aluminum foil all over the place.

There must have been a lot of horses in this outfit. Every tree of any size had a foot-deep trench around it, dug by the feet of a tied, restless horse. All of the trees in the area had been stripped bare for firewood, making it look more like a manicured county park than a wilderness area. Numerous fresh stumps remained where living trees had been cut down. Plastic insulators, nailed to trees, showed where the hunters had run an electric wire around the camp, presumably to try and hold the horses in the meadow. The discarded wire had been wadded up and thrown into a willow bush, a dangerous trap for some unsuspecting wild animal.

Although this was nothing new, I felt both sad and angry at the amount of damage a few fellow horsemen had done to this beautiful wilderness environment, probably not by intent but just out of ignorance or indifference. Unfortunately, the horse, the magnificent animal who adds so much to our wilderness adventures, is often used as the unwitting tool of degradation and destruction by those who cannot, or will not, walk into the backcountry under their own power. These callous campers use the horse as transportation, rather than for sport, not only for themselves but for their overabundant, outdated camping gear (and practices) as well.

The sad truth is, as I travel the trails through the wilderness, I find the signs of their passage over and over again. The casual disregard shown by some horse users for wilderness values is giving trail riders a bad name and is bringing all horsemen and -women on a collision course with other wilderness users. The abuses of a few shed a negative light on all of us who value riding our horses in the backcountry.

I cleaned up the hunters' camp, saddled Caluroso, and spent the rest of the day riding high into the mountains. Up there, in the foot-deep snow, where the air and the ground were all fresh and clean, my spirit soared with the peaks all around me.

I headed back to camp late in the afternoon. Coming down the trail, I ran into a group of four hunters, the first I had seen. They were all mounted, leading packhorses they were busy "reprimanding." I watched from a vantage point as they approached.

They noticed me only when their horses started whinnying to Caluroso. They told me they were turned around and were looking for a camping spot on Buck Creek. I said I knew a vacant camp and agreed to escort them to it. As we rode along, they confessed that half of their gear had fallen off their rented packhorses, coming up the trail. They were going to have to go back that afternoon and retrieve their stuff. As they started to unpack, I could see what a mess all their gear was in. They noticed me looking. One of them said, "We look like a bunch of green horns, don't we?" I didn't answer. Instead, I just wished them good luck and rode on back to my camp. But based on the way they had packed, I could already imagine what their camp would look like when they vacated it in a week or so.

I tied Caluroso out in a fresh place and made my dinner as it got dark. About an hour after I crawled into my sleeping bag, I heard the hunters coming down the trail. They were on foot, leading the packhorses. They were going back for the rest of their gear by the light of the full moon. I figured they would be cold and miserable but would probably make it all right. At four thirty the next morning I heard them come past again, grumbling and cursing, on the narrow trail above my camp. Our horses greeted each other. I welled up a "Hello, are you okay?" They hollered back, and then they were gone. I wondered what they would do if the snows came and it got really nasty?

The next day dawned clear, bright, and chilly. After a slow, easy morning savoring my solitude, I packed up and headed for home. I didn't see another soul on the trail, but as I neared the trailhead, Caluroso became very excited. Now there were at least a dozen trucks and trailers parked in the staging area, with at least fifty horses and twenty or more hunters all getting packed and ready to set off to "tame the wilderness." It looked like a Hollywood movie studio back lot. What a commotion!

I was glad I was leaving. I felt sadness, too, as I thought of the camp I had just cleaned up. I couldn't help noticing all the unnecessary paraphernalia being packed to go into the wilderness. I turned and looked back, one more time, toward the mountains and the Dark Canyon. I whispered a silent, impotent warning: *Look out, mountains! Ready or not, here they come.* 🐎

Little Elk Basin

Once you've crested the saddle that divides Trail Creek from the North Smith Fork, the drop into Little Elk Basin is steep and unrelenting. The scrub oak and serviceberry that fortify the shaley ridge top quickly give way to thick, mature stands of straight, tall, densely packed aspens. Every year there is fresh blowdown, creating an obstacle course for horse and rider to navigate. The trail goes darn near straight down. No big, lazy switchbacks here! It's as though the first brush popper who scouted the place was in a hurry to get to the bottom and make camp in the open meadows that line the creek's east side. The descent is not for the weak of limb or faint of heart.

Little Elk Basin is a quiet place, a somber place surrounded by high peaks. A subduing stillness hangs over everything. The sun drops behind the peaks early, creating a rosy alpenglow on the high mountain meadows, just above timberline. In the morning, the sun comes late, finally popping over the eastern-skyline ridge like some giant red rubber ball, instantly warming the valley that was holding its breath, shivering with expectation only moments before. At night, coyotes howl. Beavers slap their tails. Deer and elk come cautiously to drink in the many ancient, deteriorating beaver ponds. And the stars! They feel as close, and as big, as at any place on earth.

"Brush popper" is slang for a cowboy working cattle in brush.

I was anxious to see this special place once again. It was like having a rendezvous with an old friend.

You need to hobble only one horse, the one highest in the pecking order. The rest of the horses will stay near him or her.

Over the years I've camped often in this natural amphitheater. It's the perfect spot for a first night out on the trail. There's adequate feed for the horses and easy access to water, with a protective stand of dark timber to nestle a tent into. The view is spectacular, and the place feels wild and remote, especially considering it's only a three-hour ride from the trailhead.

On this particular trip, I was riding with a new friend named Lee. As our horses negotiated the last steep section of trail, I felt an excitement building in me. I was anxious to see this special place once again. It was like having a rendezvous with an old friend.

We hadn't seen any other riders on the trail, but there were fresh horse tracks, both coming in and going out. To me, it looked like four or five horses had been there the day before. I hoped we'd have the little valley to ourselves, even though there was plenty of room for numerous camps. I just like the feeling of solitude that being alone in an area gives you. So I couldn't help feeling a little disappointed when we broke out of the timber and spotted the outlines of a large, white canvas wall tent, sitting right in the center of the open meadow. I expected our horses to send a greeting to the ponies that had to be hanging out somewhere around the camp. But no . . . nothing! All was quiet.

The tent was pitched right beside the trail. To get to the other end of the meadow, where we would camp for the night, we had to ride right by it. But no one was around! The tracks coming in and going out indicated that some packers had been there the day before, setting up a hunting drop camp.

It took us only a few minutes to unpack our horses and make our camp. In a flash, our little backpack tent was set up, and water for our first course, soup, was set on the stove to boil. We had hobbled and belled one of the horses, the one higher in the pecking order, and now both of them were contentedly browsing side by side out in the meadow.

I looked beyond our horses to the large white tent, and up the hill from that, to the big, bright blue tarp, hung in a nearby stand of trees, apparently to give privacy for their camp toilet. I couldn't help feel that my own privacy had been compromised, and my enjoyment of this wilderness area violated. I decided to walk over and see what they had packed in.

Making sure no one was watching, I opened the flap and peeked inside the tent.

If you dismount and descend (or ascend) on foot, you will give your horse some relief on steep slopes.

The large wall tent was made from heavyweight canvas. It was, obviously, brand-new. It looked like it weighed a ton, and probably took one horse just to pack it in. The owners had dug a ditch all the way around it, to keep rain from coming under the bottom edge. The ridgepole and side rails were freshly cut from green aspen. Neatly stacked outside the tent was an enormous pile of firewood. A chain saw (illegal in wilderness areas) had been used to cut the logs into nice, neat, even pieces, ready to be split into firewood. I could tell it was a power saw, not a hand saw, by the size of the chips it threw out.

Now I have to admit it. In spite of myself, my curiosity got the best of me. I couldn't resist the (evil) temptation: Making sure no one was watching, I opened the flap and peeked inside the tent. The floor was covered with a carpet, of all things! Stacked in one corner, on top of a pile of aluminum fold-up cots, was a pile of thick foam mattresses. Based on the number, I figured they expected half a dozen hunters, a cook, and a wrangler. There was a brand-new metal sheepherder's stove, to heat the tent, and a four-burner gas cooking stove with a large gas bottle set in a stand, to cook on. There was also a fancy folding metal table that had a sink and dish rack built into it. I saw chuck boxes and coolers, and a half dozen folding chairs, too. I guessed that this would be the cook tent, and that the sleeping tents hadn't been packed in yet.

What an elaborate setup! And what a contrast to the simple, lightweight, compact outfit we had brought along with us, all on our riding horses! This was a hunting camp, I surmised, and these guys were going to be comfortable, no doubt about that. But at what expense to the environment? And at what sacrifice to the aesthetics of a high-quality wilderness experience? During hunting season the rules for wilderness ethics often go out the window. People seeking peace and quiet and a recreational experience vacate the backcountry when the orange army moves in and takes over. Their style of camping is as different as their reasons for being there.

As I shared the evening meal (dehydrated food made by mixing the contents of a packet with boiling water heated on a little backpacking stove) with my riding partner, I couldn't help but think out loud about the difference between these two styles of backcountry horse travel and their diametrically opposed styles of camping. My companion had been thinking the same thoughts. She was surprised at her own negative reactions to the sight of the bright blue privy and lone, white wall tent. She shared her thoughts on how this intrusion affected her relationship to the grandeur of the scene, diminishing its impact and its more soul-soothing qualities. The desired illusion, feeling like we were the first and only travelers into this wild place, had been compromised. Man, the respectful intruder, became man, the ruthless dominator. And for what? Did they really need all that stuff to stay warm, dry, and comfortable? What was going to be the quality of their wilderness experience? Or was this remote place just a setting for a bunch of good old boys to have a backwoods male-bonding party? 🐎

A MATTER OF CHOICES

None of us goes into the backcountry out of necessity. We go there by choice, for our own recreation and our own pleasure. How we go and how we treat the environment in the process affects the quality of our experience and that of other people who travel the same country after us.

One style of camping reflects the attitudes of our nation's recent history: the European immigrants conquering and taming the feared and hated wilderness. The other approach is the way of the recreation seeker: the minimalist or low-impact approach.

Civilizing the Wilderness

Not so long ago, people "domesticated" wilderness areas as they attempted to wrest a living from the land. These European invaders viewed nature as a hostile environment. They wanted to provide for themselves as many creature comforts as they could. Unlike the native people, who respected the land and saw it as their Mother, the immigrants wanted to insulate themselves from the wilderness and turn it into a more "civilized" place. The remnants of that way of thinking can still be seen in all the clever but unnecessary accouterments found in our neighbor's camp. I call this syndrome "packing the Hilton into the wilderness."

Those who follow the low-impact approach travel with as little as possible and leave all that is not essential at home. The goal is to see not how much you can bring with you, but how much you can do without. The idea is to let as little as possible get between you and your experience of the natural world. After all, it's the natural world you go out there to commune with. Instead of approaching nature with the attitude of an arrogant conqueror, a low-impact camper enjoys nature with an attitude of respect bordering on reverence.

For many, this is an exciting new way of looking at things, a link to something lost but not forgotten. For some, it is still totally foreign, fraught with suspicion that is often expressed in disdain and ridicule. But the fact is that times are changing. As more and more people turn to the outdoors to find balance and harmony and communion with the source of their existence, it becomes more important to address environmental impact concerns. That way, everyone can experience the wilderness qualities they are looking for. Our goal is to preserve, not to destroy, the wilderness we seek.

I hope that we are a long way from shutting all horse users out of wilderness and wild places. Still, more and more people want to use less and less land. As pressure from users mounts, we must ask ourselves the hard questions, look for new answers, and explore ways to reduce horse and rider impact to a minimum. By joining forces with others who are already environmentally concerned, instead of bucking the tide and isolating ourselves, we can increase our clout and strengthen our position. Obviously, the most effective way to do this is (whenever possible) to use only one horse for one rider, with the rider packing all necessary equipment on the riding horse.

Low-impact horse camping is the ultimate challenge in horse packing. It's the most environmentally friendly. And, it's fun!

CHAPTER TWO

Planning for Adventure

STORM RIDER

he day had started out peacefully enough. The night before, I had found a cozy little campsite just as dusk settled in. It was out of the wind, sheltered by a small hill, and surrounded by a grove of mature aspens whose leaves had already turned a warm golden red. A large, gently sloping meadow led down to a small, no-name stream, hidden from view by the stunted willows that grew in thick profusion along its shallow banks. Even though I had camped with the setting sun at my back, it was almost eight o'clock the next morning before rays of sunlight descended through the trees and found my tent, warming me from the outside in. I waited a while longer, enjoying this little moment of luxury, hunkered down in my cozy sleeping bag.

Earlier, at first light, I had gotten up, hobbled and belled my horse, and turned him loose from his night high line. Then I had slipped back into my cozy bag. I brewed and slowly sipped three cups of coffee and ate my bowl of steaming hot oatmeal as I enjoyed peeking out of the tent flap, watching the horse graze. It was pure pleasure, just lying there, letting my mind drift freely, and feeling the rhythm of the mountains settling into me. Finally, I broke camp, packed up, and hit the trail.

Storm clouds began to gather out of nowhere. The temperature began to drop. I hurried a little faster, feeling a strange nervousness in my horse and in myself.

Now it was midafternoon. The trail had led me higher and higher up a mountain range. Aspen groves gave way to stands of spruce and fir which, as I ascended, diminished in size from towering giants to tiny dwarfs. Now even the last holdouts, isolated, twisted stands of ancient, weathered bristlecone pines, had disappeared a thousand feet below.

The trail picked its way up easily through the slide rock, gaining altitude at a gentle angle. Long, gray granite scree slopes reached up toward the horizon in wide bands, divided by narrow corridors of low-growing shrubbery. A mile or so ahead, the trail crossed over the range at a low spot, a natural gateway in a 12,000-foot-high ridge that looked as though a row of giant pyramids had been stacked carefully along its top, making an intimidating fortress.

Storm clouds began to gather overhead, out of nowhere. Suddenly the temperature began to drop. I hurried a little faster, feeling a strange nervousness in my horse and in myself. It's amazing how quickly things can change in the high mountains. A few moments before, the sun had been shining. Now the clouds got darker and began to race toward each other as if they knew that by joining forces they could increase their threatening power. I pushed on a little faster, hoping to get across the pass before the storm struck.

I almost made it, too. Just as I broke over the crest, a ghost-like whine sent a shiver through my body and chilled me to my bones. My horse's mane stood straight up. You could feel the electricity in the air. Lightning crashed on the peaks all around me. The smell of ozone, unmistakable and pungent to the nose, filled my lungs. I stopped just long enough to tighten my cinch, pull on all my extra clothes and waterproof riding coat, and give a quick check to the trail below.

With no further ado, we started down. The trail was much steeper on this side of the range. It led precariously over a bare, exposed cliff face. Only a narrow, serpentlike series of switchbacks, probably blasted out by gold and silver miners, allowed passage to the giant glacial bowl and scattered clumps of black timber that lay thousands of feet below.

We looked like a couple of steam engines chugging down the trail.

Five hundred feet off the top, the rain hit hard. It came full force in a gust of wind so strong it almost blew me off my horse. I grabbed my hat just in the nick of time before it became a flying saucer. I pulled it down tight until it bent the top of my ears out at a crazy angle. The rain came harder and harder from every direction. Within minutes I was soaked through and through. The collar of my slicker wasn't high enough to keep the rain out. Soon a steady stream ran down the middle of my back and split in two where my posterior met my saddle, continuing on down my legs and slowly filling my boots. I started to shiver uncontrollably. Even so, I had to laugh to myself, thinking how much like a drowned rat I must have looked. I've got to tell you, I was miserable.

The rain began to let up a little. Hail and sleet took its place. The trail, bone-dry and hard as a rock only minutes before, became a slick river of mud and ice. Little white balls of melting sleet started building up under my horse's feet. The temperature kept dropping. I couldn't tell who was shivering more, my horse or me. Our breath condensed, creating puffy clouds in the frigid air. We looked like a couple of steam engines chugging down the trail.

An hour later, so cold and stiff I could barely step down from the saddle, I pulled up at the first thick stand of blue spruce we came to. I had to look at my hands and force them to move to get my gear unpacked and my horse unsaddled. I scraped away six inches of snow that had already accumulated on the soft bed of needles, and I somehow managed to set up my little tent. I shed my soaking wet clothing, crawled into my sleeping bag, and fired up my backpacking stove.

Within minutes the tent was warm and cozy. Melted snow was boiling in my pot. A cup of instant soup brought life back to my slightly hypothermic core temperature as the steaming cup warmed my hands and my spirits. It felt great to be alive!

All night long, the storm raged and buffeted my tent, but I was warm and dry inside. Periodically, I crawled out to check on my horse and move him to a fresh grazing spot. By morning the clouds had already blown away. Once again, the sun shone bright and clear. I took my time drying my clothing and gear, enjoying the luxurious warmth and the incredible view. Then I headed on down into the protection of lower country.

I have three major rules on which I base my definition of success: I must survive, my horse must survive, and I must have fun!

As I RODE DOWN THE TRAIL, I thought about the unexpected predicament I had just survived. What might easily have become a life or death experience turned out to be nothing more than a fast-fading memory, some brief discomfort, rewarded by a sense of high adventure. I mentally evaluated my clothing and equipment. I realized that if I hadn't made the right choices and packed the right stuff, I might have easily fallen victim to hypothermia. What had I done right? What could I improve? What could I learn from my experience?

These questions are always on my mind as I prepare for the next excursion into the backcountry. An adventure is a trip in which you don't know what the outcome will be. Sometimes, however, the full appreciation of the fun had on a trip takes a little time to ripen! 🐎

PREPARING FOR THE TRAIL

One of the first and most important lessons I learned back in the Boy Scouts was to follow the Scout motto "Be prepared." It didn't take too many wet, cold, and miserable camping trips to reinforce that lesson thoroughly.

A positive attitude (choosing to focus on the lesson learned instead of on the miserable experience) makes life a more joyful process, a gift to be enjoyed instead of a curse to be endured. Most lessons are learned not from our successes but from our failures. Usually the lessons help us meet our future challenges with greater success. To quote the Prophet Muhammad, "Trust in Allah, but tie up your camel." This is sound advice, not just in the desert but in any part of the world. And it's especially valuable if you are dealing with horses.

The Adventure of Life

To get the most from life, one must first come to grips with the fact that it is an adventure. My definition of the word "adventure" is a trip in which you do not know what you will encounter. Anyone who has been around horses for a long time has probably come to realize that by my definition, every ride on a horse is an

At the end of winter, I get ready to lunge Soledad before riding her.

adventure. Perhaps that is why horses give so much joy to those of us who seek adventure and share our lives with them. They take us out of the humdrum world that we as a society have created for ourselves. They take us back a step to a world where we are in touch with nature and help us realize that we are a part of, not separate from, nature. But, and there is always a but, let's face it: as much as we love them, horses (and riding) are dangerous!

Horses are large, powerful herd animals whose natural instincts are to run, buck, kick, or bite when they perceive or interpret danger. Usually this instinctive reflex far overshadows their ability to stop and reason. Under the right (or wrong) conditions, a fluttering piece of paper can scream a message to their brains, "Sabertoothed tiger!" Without warning, horse and rider may be "off to the races" with uncertain and possibly unpleasant consequences. So before you go for that next ride, think for a moment about the unscheduled events that might present themselves. You might find it worthwhile to do a little pre-ride preparation and exercise the seven Ps that I was taught in the Marine Corps: Proper prior planning prevents

predictably poor performance. Be a good Scout and securely tie up your camel (or horse), just in case.

Top: Lunging helps to work the kinks out and re-establish a working relationship after months or weeks of pasture time. Bottom: I ride bareback for most of my training and conditioning work with horses.

DON'S DAILY DOZEN

The more in shape you are, the more you'll enjoy riding, and the more your horse will enjoy you! Staying in reasonable shape and keeping yourself down to a healthy weight just makes good sense.

So here's Don's Daily Dozen (Baker's Dozen), exercises to get you going and keep you going, moving toward mastery of your mind, body, and spirit. Doing them once won't help! Only by exercising every day, as part of your chosen lifestyle, will you achieve the benefits hidden inside these thirteen simple exercises. Don't wait — begin now!

1. Dog stretches

2. Salutation to the sun

3. Picking apples

4. Side stretches

5. Opposite toe touches

6. Elbow back thrusts

7. Side-to-side karate stretch

8. Telemark leg thrusts

9. High kicks

10. Leg lifts

11. Sit-ups

12. Push-ups

13. Relax and breathe

A HORSEMAN'S "POSSIBLES"

Years ago, as a teenager, I was captivated by a story about an independent mountain man who braved the elements and tested his skills in the wildest country.

He traveled with only his horse for transportation and companionship. He had a well-selected kit of essentials, things that he could easily carry in an over-the-shoulder bag. These items he called his "Possibles."

This pure, self-reliant form of adventure held a strong appeal for me, one that has not faded with time. Over the years it has become the unifying thread, woven through the fabric of my existence, that has clothed the framework of my life. True, I live in another age and another time from my mountain man hero. I don't have to kill deer to feed the hunger in my belly. Instead, I stalk and study all of nature to feed the hunger in my soul. Through my many mini-adventures on horseback, I regularly revisit the places that reconnect me to the Mother Earth and the spirit of the universe.

Over the years, I have accumulated my own Possibles — small items I habitually take along, wherever I go. I have found them useful in making my adventures more pleasant, more comfortable, and safer. In some instances, they have even saved my life or the life of my horse. My Possibles are my personal survival kit.

The Right Knife

The first and perhaps most important single item, one that I wouldn't go near a horse without having close at hand, is a knife. Knives are like people; they come in all shapes and sizes. When picking the right horseman's knife, try to keep in mind what you might actually use it for. You aren't Crocodile Dundee facing down punks in a New York City ghetto, John Wayne landing on the beach at Iwo Jima, or Jim Bowie fighting duels with riverboat gamblers. You probably aren't even going to skin a grizzly like David Crockett did. You'd be better off selecting a knife that can cut a small rope or spread peanut butter and jelly without injuring anyone.

The easier it is to carry without being in the way or weighing you down, the better. You are more likely to have it handy when your horse gets his lead rope snagged in a tree limb and decides to hang himself. Personally, I don't want the blade to be more than three inches long. That way, if I accidentally stab myself, it probably won't be fatal.

Other Essentials

The other Possibles are items I carry in a small nylon sack with a zipper opening. Everything stays clean but is readily accessible. Some items vary with the season, but mostly they come along for the ride just in case I need them. I have found that when I do need them, I really need them and am very happy I didn't leave home without them.

A light, unobtrusive, sturdy, stubby, lock-back folding knife that can be kept in a belt sheath fits the bill just fine.

MY LIST OF "POSSIBLES"

For your own list, add or subtract items as needed. Throw your possibles into your cantle bag along with a good windbreaker and a water bottle, and you're set to handle most of the mini-adventures that might waylay you out on the trail.

- acetaminophen (Tylenol)

- antacid such as Tums or Rolaids (balance body pH and relieve stress or dehydration symptoms such as "the jumps" in fatigued leg muscles)

- aspirin

- candle

- cigarette lighter (small for emergency fires or lighting the stove)

- codeine such as Empirin No. 3 or Tylenol No. 3 (both available only by prescription) can keep you from going into pain-related shock — from a broken arm, for example.

- dental floss (small emergency roll)

- fingernail clippers (so you don't get stuck with a terminal hang-nail)

- flashlight (mini) with lithium-powered battery (lasts for hours in any temperature)

- ibuprofen (Advil)

- insect repellent for you and your horse (I hate bugs! So does my horse!)

- iodine in a small eyedropper bottle (Put three drops in one quart of water and wait thirty minutes to kill Giardia, amoebas, grungy fungi, and any other bad stuff that might be hiding in the water.)

- liquid-filled compass (It helps a lot if you know how to use it.)

- loperamide HCl (Imodium A-D. I have discovered that diarrhea is incompatible with quality horse-back riding)

- magnifying glass (for looking for splinters in a wound, etc.)

- matches in a waterproof match case

- mirror (small, for finding a lost contact lens as well as signaling for help)

- plastic garbage bag (for emergency rain gear or to cover your saddle at night)

- safety pins, needles, and thread

- screwdriver (tiny, for fixing glasses, etc.)

- steel wool (for lighting fires in foul weather)

- sunblock 30 SPF or higher

- Swiss army knife with scissors and corkscrew for the real emergencies (such as discovering the bottle top isn't a twist-off)

- tool kit with Leatherman-type folding pliers

- whistle with neck string

- wide roll of adhesive tape and an assortment of adhesive bandages and sterile dressings

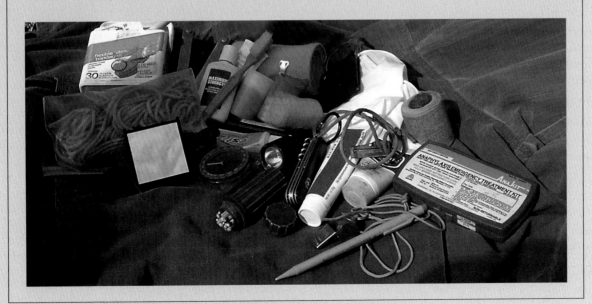

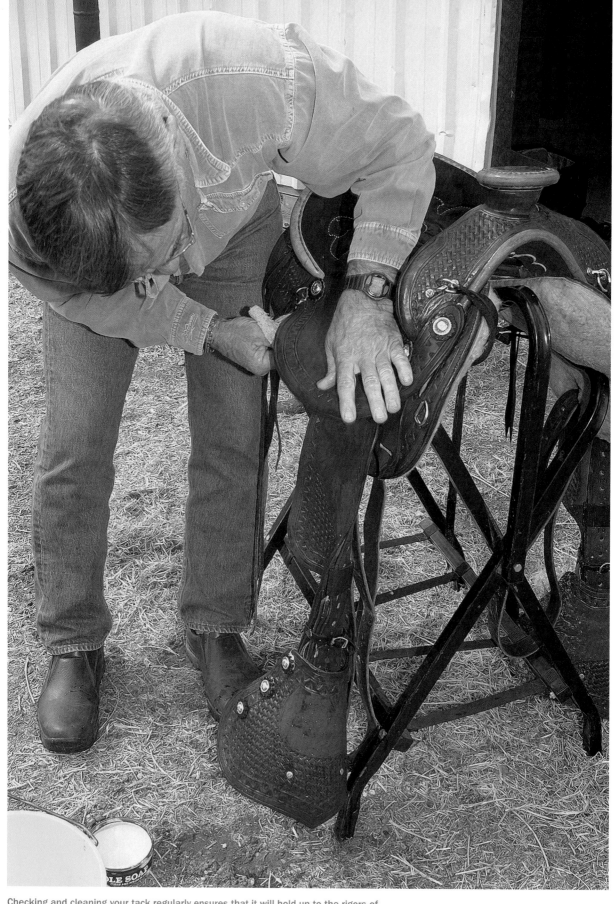

Checking and cleaning your tack regularly ensures that it will hold up to the rigors of the trail.

CAMPING GEAR

Here is a list of items that will keep you comfortable in the worst of conditions.

- bowl

- cup

- foam pad (or three-quarters-length self-inflating air mattress with short-ties to keep it rolled up)

- food (see page 47)

- fuel bottle (with a good cap) and funnel, or fuel cartridge

- paper towels

- plastic garbage bag (to cover saddle at night, etc.)

- pots (nesting) and lids with handles (in bag)

- saddle bags and cantle bags to pack gear

- salt and pepper shakers (waterproof)

- sleeping bag and waterproof stuff sack (lightweight backpacking type — no more than three pounds)

- soap (liquid biodegradable) and sponge with scrubbing pad

- spoons

- toilet paper and premoistened wipes in zip closure bag (plus tiny bottle of bleach to disinfect hands)

- ultralight backpacking stove, cigarette lighter, and funnel (in bag)

- ultralight tent and fly plus poles and stakes (no more than three pounds per person)

- water bottles (bicycle type)

Above: A good secure tent and fly, a dry sleeping bag, a three-quarter-length foam pad, a small stove, and a pot along with a waterproof collapsible bucket, saddle-bags, and cantle bag, are all critical to success when Mother Nature shows her nasty side. Below: My "possibles" bag.

YOUR WILDERNESS WARDROBE

Making the right choices in clothing is very important. At the very least, these choices affect your comfort and enjoyment on any wilderness foray.

The smart wilderness traveler plans and packs his or her wardrobe as though life depended upon it. After all, it just might!

Let's start with long underwear. Don't use cotton. Cotton is fine for riding in the car or sitting and sipping cappuccino in a cafe. But when your life depends on staying warm and dry, cotton is the worst choice. It's a natural fiber that absorbs moisture and requires energy in the form of heat — yours — to dry it out. When I was younger, I wore 100 percent natural wool long underwear, but now the synthetic fibers are so good that I have lost the itch for wool. I pack light-weight polypropylene long johns, both tops and bottoms, on any overnight trip. Even if the weather behaves perfectly, they make great pajamas.

Layering is the only way to go when it comes to dressing for the backcountry. One pair of jeans and a T-shirt, polo shirt, or long-sleeved cotton shirt, along with a lightweight polypropylene undershirt, make the ideal outfit for fair-weather riding. As things deteriorate, add a warm vest, a nylon windbreaker, and a polar fleece jacket in any combination that meets your needs.

A bandana will keep a cold breeze from chilling your neck. A hat is a must. You can lose as much as 30 percent of your body heat through your head. I usually take a baseball cap and a fleece stocking cap. The first shades my face and eyes from the sun. The second keeps me warm when an unexpected storm catches me out in the high country or when I'm chilly when I first hit the sleeping bag.

A wind- and water-repellent outer layer is absolutely critical. Don't leave home without one! I choose a three-quarter-

---

PERSONAL CLOTHING

• chinks (waterproof and breathable nylon)

• gaiters (waterproof and breathable nylon)

• gloves

• helmet or cowboy hat

• jeans

• long underwear (light- or medium-weight polypropylene or equivalent)

• neckerchief

• riding coat (waterproof or very water resistant and breathable)

• shirt, long-sleeved (cotton, synthetic, or lightweight wool, depending on conditions)

• shirt, short-sleeved (polo shirt or T-shirt)

• shoes, boots, or riding sneakers (something you can lace up and really walk in)

• socks (wool, polypropylene, or mixture) — two pairs

• stocking cap

• vest

• undershorts (cotton or synthetic)

• windbreaker

• wool sweater or fleece jacket (medium weight for layering)

PERSONAL ITEMS

• camera and film (compact)

• field glasses (compact)

• folding knife (in belt sheath)

• glasses and sunglasses (with case)

• headlamp

• insect repellent

• small washcloth

• sunscreen

• toilet paper (in sealed plastic bag)

• toothbrush

• toothpaste

length riding jacket made of waterproof, breathable Cordura-Supplex nylon, as opposed to the currently popular oiled cotton duster-length coats, for most trips. Long coats may look fashionable, but they make getting on and off a horse an adventure in itself, especially in a big blow. When a horse is already rattled and you're on a narrow trail, a coat that's billowing out and blowing up in the air can be the final blow . . . literally. Trying to walk up a steep hill, always stepping on its front hem, can be downright exasperating, too! So I choose a coat that's long enough to surround my saddle and keep water from running down the inside of my cantle. A very high collar, a hood, long sleeves to cover your hands, and hand-warmer pockets are all priceless features when you need them the most.

A pair of short chaps, called chinks, fills the gap between the coat and gaiters (adjustable leggings) and keeps your jeans dry. Gaiters (also called half chaps) are lighter and more versatile than high boots. Both my chinks and gaiters are made of waterproof, breathable Cordura nylon. Nylon is lighter than leather, stuffs away easily, doesn't absorb moisture, keeps you dryer, and gives you more freedom of movement.

It's great to look like the Marlboro man at the Saturday night dance, but in the backcountry, high-heeled cowboy boots can be a real hazard. I find that a good pair of lightweight, sturdy, low-heeled, lace-up boots with a shallow treaded sole are the best. They give you support for riding and are a must if you want to get down and walk.

Throw in a few pairs of poly-wool socks and fleece gloves, and you're ready to take on almost any weather condition.

Your clothing should be light, sturdy, waterproof, and breathable.

PLANNING FOR A LOW-IMPACT HORSE CAMPING TRIP

Half the fun of any trip is the anticipation and the planning. My friends and I spend weeks poring over topographical maps of Colorado's West Elk Wilderness Area, imagining where we will camp, going over our menu with active (heated) discussions about what we will eat on what night, and, of course, who will do the cooking.

Seeing all the gear spread out on the floor, with piles of stuff thrown here and there, it is hard to believe that it is somehow all going to fit into our saddle and cantle bags, to be carried by our trusty riding horses, along with us!

Our objective is to inspect all the equipment and to reduce it to the minimum weight and volume that will still give us a reasonable margin of safety and comfort. Now is the time to scrutinize each item, to decide if it is in or out. We all abide by one basic rule: When in doubt, leave it out. By traveling light we can eliminate the need for packhorses, save extra work and hassles, and allow ourselves more freedom. In the process, we will cause far less damage to the fragile mountain environment, leaving it looking untouched for others to enjoy, just the way we found it.

We start by looking over the tack and equipment we are going to need for our horses. Of course, each horse and rider have their own saddle. The importance of this piece of gear cannot be overemphasized. The more weight a horse is expected to carry, the more critical good saddle fit becomes. The bars of each saddletree should make even contact along both sides of a horse's back, not create any sore spots, and spread the load over the maximum weight-bearing area. Naturally, the lighter the saddle, the better.

Each horse has a thick, clean, synthetic fleece saddle pad, with foam inserts where the saddletree bars meet the horse's back. Synthetic materials wick sweat away from a horse's back without retaining moisture, keeping the horse dry and comfortable and helping to reduce the possibility of developing sores. They also dry out more quickly than wool or wool felt. I now always use an orthopedic pad, made with special foam inserts under the bars, with good results.

Each saddle is fitted with a crupper (a leather loop that passes under a horse's tail and is buckled to the saddle). When a horse goes downhill it automatically tucks its tail under itself, thus tightening the crupper, keeping the front of the saddletree bars from bumping or riding up and over the horse's shoulders with every step. The long downhill sections are where a horse is most vulnerable to sore muscles and related injuries.

The crupper helps keep the saddle from shifting forward on steep descents.

Lightweight, comfortable breast collars are also a must. They keep the saddle from sliding back on steep uphill pulls. Our saddles are equipped with a set of specially designed *tapadero*-style stirrups, with full floor, to keep the rider's foot from getting hung up and eliminate the need for high-heeled boots.

All the leather gear is freshly saddle soaped and lightly oiled (we use olive oil) and then carefully inspected for weaknesses that might cause an accident or require a difficult repair out in the backcountry.

Each horse has its own nylon halter and lead rope.

A tapadero is a toe fender (a leather strap in front of the stirrup) that protects the rider's toe from getting caught in brush.

Clockwise from left: crupper, bosal with reins, synthtic saddle pad, woven breast collar and girth, and nylon lead rope.

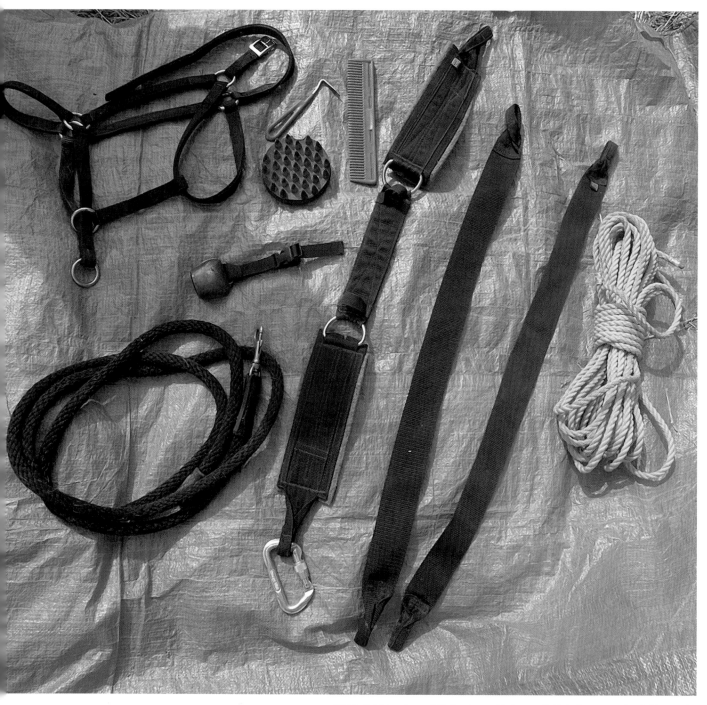

Clockwise from lower left: lead rope, Swiss cowbell, halter, curry, hoofpick, comb, hobbles, tree-saver straps, and nylon rope.

A small Swiss cowbell, attached to the throat strap of the halter at turnout time, is insurance against a lost horse. Comfortable, lightweight hobbles, a locking aluminum rock-climbing carabiner, two tree-saver straps, and fifty feet of yellow polypropylene rope round out our tie-out gear. A properly fitted headset, including bridle, bit or bosal, and reins, complete the outfit.

We all take a few pounds of oats for horse treats. Treats help keep the horses hanging around camp, looking for more.

Personal items and clothing make up another pile. We each check the items off our list. In a little group pile we have a small bottle of biodegradable soap, a small plastic bottle of bleach, a large first aid kit, a fix-it kit, and, of course, the maps and compass.

Food, Glorious Food

All our cooking is done on an ultralightweight backpacking stove. Each person has a spoon, cup, and bowl. They nestle nicely into a nesting stainless-steel pot-and-pan set. One quart of fuel in an aluminum fuel bottle or the appropriate number of fuel canisters ensure enough cooking power for a three-day trip. A cigarette lighter stored in the pot set makes lighting the stove easy.

TYPICAL MENUS

BREAKFAST

- brown sugar
- coffee or tea
- dried fruit
- granola
- honey
- hot oatmeal (individual packets)
- hot or cold powdered juice (e.g., Tang)
- margarine
- powdered milk
- raisins
- white sugar

LUNCH

- bagels
- cheese
- cream cheese
- dried fruit
- energy or granola bars
- gorp (Good Old Raisins and Peanuts: a mix of nuts, dried fruit, carob bits, etc.)
- jam or jelly
- powdered drinks (e.g., Crystal Light, Gatorade)

DINNER

- instant soup (individual packets)
- main course: many good dehydrated meals are available; add boiling water and let simmer, then add cheese, margarine, powdered milk, salt, and pepper
- dessert: instant pudding, dehydrated applesauce, etc.
- hot drinks: hot chocolate, tea, coffee, or hot Tang

Our meals consist mostly of dehydrated food, in order to save on weight and bulk; no heavy cans or fresh stuff (except for the hamburger and onion I'll smuggle in for the first night's spaghetti dinner). Salt and pepper and some favorite spices add a lot to the palatability of camp meals. And a fresh, steaming hot cup of coffee, made with a one-cup filter, can ease the transition from the world of dreams to another day in the saddle with a certain degree of civility.

Packing Our Bags

Finally we have everything sorted out. All we have to do now is pack it. The clothing we won't be wearing, along with other soft, compressible

Dehydrated camping meals have come a long way and don't taste all that bad, especially after a long day in the saddle!

items, such as sleeping bag, part of the tent, and foam pad, all go into the cantle bag. This will ride on the horse's back, behind the saddle, without doing any damage or causing discomfort. Pots and pans, stove and fuel bottle, food, and all the group gear are divided by weight and bulk and carefully stack-loaded into our well-padded saddlebags. Water bottles, munchies, lunch for the trail, and such personal items as cameras are kept close at hand in pommel bags. This way, we won't

I don't pack food for my horse in the backcountry. I plan my low-impact overnight trips when I know there will be adequate natural feed available. Out on the trail I stop often and let my horse graze as I gaze. If you need to take feed for your horse you will need to pack a packhorse. If you are going to pack feed, pack certified weed-free dehydrated feed.

Above: Packed up and ready to go!
Below: Ready to ride and prepared for stormy weather.

have to stop and dismount to get a quick drink or a snack.

By the time we have everything packed and the compression straps cinched down on the load, it doesn't look so bad after all! Although each horse will carry about fifty pounds of gear (including saddle and tack), it will be distributed so that it causes the horse the least discomfort possible. We run through our checklist one last time. Have we forgotten anything or taken something we can do without?

Everything seems to be in order. Tomorrow we'll be off on our own horseback adventure.

HELMETS

Let me state for the record that I think it is smart to wear a safety helmet. I expect to see more and more people using them in the future, as fashion gives way to function. They will save lives, no doubt, and will probably save even more headaches than heartaches.

Pickets, Bells, and Hobbles

My dog Nicky is always ready for adventure.

I sat quietly astride my horse, on the top of a small grassy knoll, looking out over the mountains and watching the sun drop down and disappear behind the horizon. The soft light of alpenglow momentarily lingered on the highest peaks. Witnessing the turning of the aspen leaves shimmering in the glory of their golden and red grand finale and breathing in the smell of autumn in the high-country air sent my mind off on a nostalgic journey, back to another September long ago. It had been almost twenty-five years since I had made my first solo horse camping trip. Still, I remembered it clearly, as though it were just the other day.

In preparation, I had devoured the few horse-packing books I could get my hands on. I'd asked questions of those I thought might know. But mostly I was relying on my own years of experience with both horses and camping, learned in the school of hard knocks (now more fashionably referred to by educators as "experiential learning"). Finally, the time had come. With my horse Cindy and my dog Nicky, I set off into the mountains of Colorado to test my skills . . . and my sense of humor.

I rode for a long time that first day. The air was crisp and cool. The sun shone brightly in an azure sky, with only an occasional cloud drifting overhead. I covered eight or nine miles, mostly uphill, from the trailhead to a grassy clearing in a dark timber-lined mountain valley. I sat alone by my little campfire that evening, enjoying my solitude and my last cup of coffee. I watched in awe as the sky, as though drained of color, faded quickly from gray to black. Crystal clear stars popped out of nowhere and twinkled in numbers beyond belief. The scene freed me from my earthbound perspective, giving me a sense of my own insignificance in this vast universe. I indulged myself in the feeling of satisfaction I experienced, having completed my first day on the trail with no major messups or mishaps. This was going to be easy!

At about two o'clock that morning, Nicky started barking furiously. I stuck my head out of the tent just in time to see him chasing a large black bear back into the timber. I supposed the bear had come around to check out the goodies in my camp larder! Or maybe he was just lonely and wanted some company. But now he was gone and so was my horse.

I pulled on my jeans and went to search for my horse. Cindy, my trusty sorrel quarter-mustang mare, had been staked out in the clearing near my tent where I could keep an eye on her. For this first trip, I had bought a brand-new metal picket pin that

Now the bear was gone and so was my horse.

Cindy's hoofprints led me eight miles down to the trailhead, where she was waiting, ready to go home.

looked like a giant corkscrew and a leather one-leg hobble. I had joined them together with thirty feet of hemp rope. Where moments before she had been securely anchored, I found a broken hobble, a tangled rope, and the picket pin. The pin had been jerked out of the ground so forcefully that it had lost its curl and now looked like a long spear. But there was no Cindy. She was long gone. Feeling suddenly alone and humbled, I crawled back into the security of my tent and waited impatiently for the morning. As they say, tomorrow is another day.

With first light, I was able to pick up her tracks. They were easy enough to read on this little-used trail. I packed a water bottle, some food, and my jean jacket, and started tracking her. She had headed back down the trail the way we had come up the day before. After a few miles of walking, my feet started to get hot, sweaty, and really sore. I could feel blisters developing inside my fancy black, pointy-toed, high-heeled cowboy boots. My head was sweating under my broad-brimmed, black cowboy hat. Right then, I would have killed for a pair of sneakers and a baseball cap. Truth is, I was developing a monster headache, too.

About a mile or so farther back down the trail, there was a drift fence where I had come through a closed gate. I figured I'd find Cindy there, but, as I approached, I was disappointed. No horse. Instead, her tracks turned and went up along the fence line a ways, then disappeared. I doubled back to the trail and went through the gate. Sure enough, there were her tracks again. She must have jumped the fence. I looked for signs of blood, but, to my relief, I couldn't find any. I only hoped she hadn't hurt herself crossing the barbed wire.

Finally, the trail broke out of the timber. From this high vantage point I could see my truck and trailer parked next to a run-down cow camp in the open valley bottom a mile or so below. Next to the trailer, I made out a brown spot. It moved. Sure enough, it was my old mare Cindy, contentedly munching grass and waiting for me to take her home. I wanted to go home, too, but now my camp was eight miles up the mountain! After nursing my crippled feet in the cool stream, I tied my boots together, slung them over Cindy's back, climbed onboard bareback (and barefoot), and headed up the trail, back to my high camp. The day before, I had started my adventure looking like a silver screen cowboy. Now, only one day later, tired and dirty, I looked more like a plowboy. So much for image!

I believe that life loves you so much that it keeps bringing you the same lessons over and over again until you learn from them. On this particular issue, I felt I had learned enough for one trip. That night, I took no chances. I tied the mare's lead rope to a second rope strung high up between two trees. As I reflected on the events of the day, I was thankful that Cindy had not been hurt. I was sore-bottomed and bowlegged, but no worse for wear. Except for the half-dollar-sized blisters on my toes and heels, I was still okay. Perhaps horse camping was not so easy after all! Sitting alone by my campsite I acknowledged to myself that I still had a lot to learn. 🐎

Above: A high line like this one is the best way to secure your horse. Left: I set up my tent in a mountain meadow.

HOW NOT TO LOSE YOUR HORSE

When I think about horse camping, nothing is more sobering to me than the thought of being a few days out in the backcountry and losing my horse.

To wake up in the morning and not see my horse where I left him or her the night before brings thoughts of desperate searches, long walks, even finding the horse injured or dead. With some knowledge and some pretrip lessons about pickets, bells, and hobbles for the horse, these unpleasant scenarios can almost always be avoided. I have done some experimenting over the years (once again, in the school of hard knocks). Here are a few of the solutions I've come up with. They work for me. Maybe they'll work for you, too.

First, I look for a place to camp that has plenty of feed for my horses, water within easy walking distance, a good view (for me), and a lot of space for the horses to drift around and forage where I can still keep an eye on them. I try to make camp by late afternoon, to allow plenty of time for my horses to graze, while I set up my tent. As soon as the horses are unpacked and unsaddled, I take them off a ways, where they won't be a nuisance, bell them, hobble one of them (the leader), and turn them loose. After a day on the trail, they're usually content to eat and visit with their buddies.

I tie a small Swiss cowbell either to the halter or on a separate neck strap of each horse to keep track of the horses' whereabouts. Don't tie the bell down where the lead rope attaches to your halter. It'll interfere with the horse's eating and ring furiously all the time. If you tie it up under the throatlatch, it'll ring only when the horse moves abruptly or if he gets himself hung up and is in trouble. Although the bells may be a bit of a nuisance around camp, you'll get to where you can interpret their ringing, even in your sleep. They sure make finding a loose horse who has wandered off a heck of a lot easier.

Using Hobbles

I prefer nylon hobbles. They are lighter than leather and don't stretch when they get wet. I make some that are two inches wide and padded with felt to protect the soft skin around your horse's pasterns. There are a lot of cheap hobbles on the market. Unfortunately, most of them are too narrow and tend to sore a horse quickly. Avoid them.

Horses who are accustomed to hobbles can travel amazing distances in the course of a night. A hobble's primary function is merely to slow your horse down so you can catch him on foot. So don't depend on hobbles alone to keep your horses around camp when you can't keep an eye on them.

The cowbell strap should be lightweight so that it breaks if caught in brush.

Left: Put the hobbles on the front legs, low, around the pastern. They don't have to be really tight. Below: After a long day on the trail, the horses are usually happy to graze nearby.

A night high line is the most environmentally friendly method of tying your horse. Look for two trees with thirty to forty feet of open, grassy ground between them.

Tying Out

At night, to be sure I am riding and not walking the next day, I tie my horses out, but not just to a tree. Horses left tied to a tree get restless and can do a lot of walking. They can paw and dig a ditch around the tree, injuring its roots and possibly killing it or at least leaving an unsightly area.

If you do have to picket your horse (tie him directly to a fixed line), make sure the anchor is securely fastened, or heavy enough that the horse will not be able to pull it around easily. A spooked horse dragging around a small log can cause a big wreck in short order. When picketing an inexperienced horse, tie the picket line to the halter and leave the horse hobbled. That way he cannot run to the end of the picket line and hurt himself.

Things are a little easier when you travel with a group, as opposed to traveling alone. Horses, like most people, enjoy company, and when their work is done, they like hanging out together. By observing their pecking order, you'll soon see who the boss horses are. Hobbling or tying the leaders usually keeps the others close at hand.

To get Soledad used to the feel of hobbles, I use a long soft lunge rope and gently run it around her legs and pasterns. Gradually I ask her to lift her leg by applying pressure to one leg and then the other.

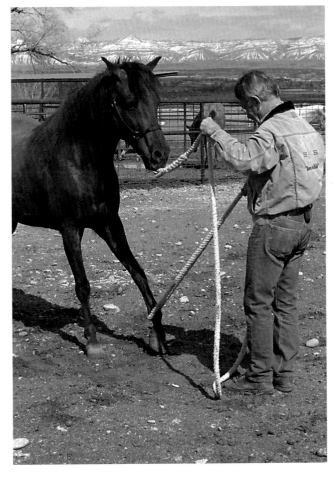

NIGHT RESTRAINT: HIGH LINE

The less a horse is physically restrained, the less damage he does to the environment. A free horse does less harm than a tied horse. With this in mind, the best way to handle horses at night, on an overnight trip, is to tie them out on a night line.

Select two sturdy trees with open ground between them, about thirty to forty feet apart. Try to pick a place where a little trampling by your horse won't leave a permanent scar or cause erosion. A flat, open place with plenty of grass is best. If the same spot is not used over and over again, it will usually recover quickly. To protect the tree's cambium layer (the living layer where cell growth takes place right below the bark), use tree-saver straps. Two-inch-wide nylon or polypropylene webbing does a great job. Use a piece about a yard long, with an eye tied or sewed into each end. These lightweight tree savers protect the trees from unnecessary rope burn.

Run your tree-saver strap around the tree, up high, as high as you can reach, plus some. Take a fifty-foot-long piece of polypropylene rope and tie it through the eyes in one end of the tree-saver strap (after you put the strap around the tree). A bowline knot works great and is easy to untie, even after it's been under pressure. Now, put another tree-saver strap around the other tree you plan to use. Stretch your night line between them. Once again, get the strap as high as you can reach. Run the other end of your polypropylene rope through the loops in the second tree saver. Now pull it up, really tight, and tie it.

Attach your night line to the tree as high as you can reach.

A bowline is a good knot to use and is easy to untie.

TYING YOUR HORSE TO THE NIGHTLINE

Put a figure eight in the end of your lead rope. Allow your horse enough slack to reach the ground to eat, without making it easy for him to step over the rope and get tangled. Use a carabiner with a locking gate to secure the lead line to the night line.

Set your night lines up so your horses can all see each other but can't tangle themselves with each other. Leave the horses on the night line as little as possible. The rest of the time they can be hobbled and left to roam around to graze and socialize as you enjoy camp.

To keep your horse from walking around the tree (on either end of your high line), tie an eight-inch-long stick in the night line about five feet from the tree on either end, using a clove hitch, before you pull it up tight. This will confine the carabiners to the central part of the rope and stop the horse from going around the tree.

Here's a good way to get the night line stretched really tight. Tie one end of your rope to the tree saver with a bow-line. After putting the other end through the loops in the second tree saver, come back along the part of the rope to be stretched. Tie a figure eight knot in this part of the rope, about two feet away from the tree. You'll have a loop (or an eye) at the end of the figure eight. This will act as a pulley that makes it easy to tighten your line.

On Top of the World

Every trip has its special moments, those little events that come along when least expected, to make an otherwise routine experience live repeatedly in your memory. As time consumes the details of day-to-day events, these mental daggers keep a fresh edge and maintain their sharpness. Let me give you one personal example so you'll understand what I'm talking about.

I had been with my clients for two days (and nights), almost full-time. Although they were interesting people and had been great company, I was looking forward to a little escape into my own private space. In short, I needed some time alone.

We had made a high camp, right below timberline, where a group of ancient spruce trees stood tall like sentinels guarding the small pass, crowded in by two 13,000-foot peaks that towered like citadel spires above. A side valley, carved into the larger of the two mountains by ages of glaciers that receded 10,000 years ago, provided a foothold for a meadow with a little stream meandering through it. Farther up the ever-steepening hillsides, the native grasses reluctantly gave way to thick groves of aspen. Above that, nothing but huge boulder fields of granite blocks, piled helter-skelter on top of each other, covered the mountainside. They could be seen running up to the skyline like giant metallic fingers, as though a steel-gloved hand had reached down and crushed the stunted spruce trees that clung to the well-defined ridgelines.

My plan was to get up before dawn, climb up one of these talus slopes, and have a world-class view of the land that fell away at my feet; a mini-solo for sunrise. And, that was exactly what I did! The moon had dropped down below the horizon off in the west a few hours earlier. In the heavy, nearly absolute darkness that preceded the dawn, the stars glittered in the sky as though a black blanket had been riddled with pinholes and thrown over the earth with a brilliant light source behind it. I headed into the darkness with confidence. I had planned (and carefully studied) my route the evening before. Just as I had imagined, it was fairly easygoing — at first. Huge blocks of granite, unmoved for eons, trundled under my weight. They made a deep, growly noise as they shifted their position. Sometimes their movement created enough friction to release ozone. The unmistakable smell came wafting up to fill my nostrils, an interesting but seemingly out-of-place aroma.

As I climbed higher, my route became steeper. The boulders diminished in size until I was walking on a stack of dinner-plate-sized slabs that made a clattering sound as they rearranged themselves under my feet with every step. I let my intuition be my guide. Having no destination in mind, I just searched for a place that felt right — my perfect spot. At last, I was alone and at peace.

I didn't have to go far to find my private paradise. I was only fifteen minutes out of camp, but still I felt as though I was in a different, separate universe. I sat down and just let the peace and quiet sink into me. Already, streaks of color were starting to show on the eastern horizon. The skyline began to shimmer. First light was only minutes away.

As I sat there, eyes closed, breathing deeply, lost in my own reverie, waiting, I enjoyed the feel of the shifting breezes caressing my face through the darkness. Then, unexpectedly, another smell came floating out of the darkness. It was not ozone; what was it? Almost indistinguishable, like a phantom, it was there for a moment and then gone. It was faint but familiar. No, I must be mistaken! That smell could not be what I thought it was. Could it? But, sure enough, there it was again.

The sun popped up abruptly like a red rubber ball. It showered the landscape with long streaks of light — an absolutely spectacular way to start the day. And in the brilliant glow that now illuminated everything, I spied, just below me, a mound of human feces with a streamer of white toilet paper stuck to its top, gently flapping in the morning breeze.

As you might guess, the magic spell was abruptly broken. I have to be honest here. I was annoyed to find in such an unaesthetic way that I was not the first person to enjoy "my spot." Those of us who appreciate the wilderness qualities of our adventures prefer to at least try to create (and maintain) the illusion that we are the first to visit the wild places we seek out. In order to foster this fantasy, we must all discipline ourselves, establish environmentally friendly policies and procedures, and practice low-impact camping techniques. Our goal should be to keep our presence and impact on the environment to a bare minimum, and to leave the wilderness looking untouched, exactly as we found it, so that someone else can enjoy it. That's the guiding principle and the challenge of low-impact horse camping. 🐎

BACKCOUNTRY ETHICS AND HYGIENE

We already know that by reducing the number of horses to a minimum, staying on the trails, and being extra careful when riding through fragile, easily trampled areas, we are practicing good backcountry horse manners.

We have talked about tying out our horses and using tree-saver straps and high lines to lower their impact. But what about the things we do ourselves? How do we reduce our own wear and

tear on the wilderness we love?

One of my favorite rules to live by says "imitate success." Our backpacking counterparts have been doing a good job and have set the standards in this department for many years. This is, at least in part, due to the fact that it is hard work to pack tools of destruction into the wild places when you have to carry them on your own back. But, in all fairness, it can also be said that the early day backpackers had a strong sense of true wilderness values and were vigilant in wanting to preserve the natural features of the environment. From them, we have inherited the mandate, and have been shown the techniques needed to take nothing but pictures and leave nothing but footprints (or hoofprints).

On the other hand, many professional guides and packers saw the wilderness through more utilitarian eyes. They were men who made their living from the land, often farmers, ranchers, and loggers who took up packing in dudes and tending to tenderfeet as an extra source of income. They viewed the

backcountry more as a commodity to be used in the spirit of taming it, rather than a sanctuary to be appreciated by preserving it.

We still see the end product of this exploitative attitude in the luxury horse pack trips that include canvas-wall tents, fold up cots, tables and chairs, foam mattresses, sheepherder's stoves, chain saws, generators for electric lights and heaters, and steak and lobster meals served ten miles from the road head (by authentic-looking cowboys). As appealing as these "city-slicker" outings may appear in glossy cowboy magazine or dude ranch pictures, portraying them as a piece of nostalgia right out of the Old West, there is a heavy price to be paid for these opulent wilderness excursions. It's not just the "dudes" that pay the price — it's the wilderness. Other wilderness users are well aware of (and getting fed up with) our bad backcountry manners.

Hygiene

So what can we do and, equally important, what shouldn't we do? Let's deal first with the business that I first alluded to, and then move on. If you plan to stay out in the backcountry for more than one day and unless you eat nothing but vitamin pills and take loperamide HCl (Imodium A-D), you will probably at some point have to make a toilet. Human feces can spread disease (as well as smell and look unpleasant). It is not unusual to find some, along with an accompanying wad of used toilet paper, under every medium-sized rock within easy walking distance of well-used campsites.

For this activity it is best to choose a site well away from camp and well away from all water. Pick an area with good soil. Dig a hole about six to eight inches deep, first carefully removing the top layer (to replace afterward). When you have completed your mission, put your toilet paper into a resealable plastic bag and either pack it out or burn it in an appropriate, safe place. When you are done, fill the hole back in. Remember, a good, long hike out of camp usually makes this a more thoroughly satisfying and solitary experience, so you don't have it cut short by an unexpected intrusion on your privacy. Take your time.

Bathing

After a day or two of traveling, another consideration might be how to take a bath.

Don't go down to the beaver pond with your soap and shampoo, jump in, and lather up. Even biodegradable soap contaminates streams and lakes. The best method for washing yourself is to heat a few pots of water on your stove, go well away from the stream, wash yourself with a little washcloth, and then rinse off with the warm water. Then, when you are clean, if you still want to swim, have at it. Usually, at least in the mountains (unless you're a polar bear), you won't stay in very long.

Washing Dishes

Dishes should be washed the same way, that is, well away from the stream site. Finding strands of the spaghetti the last traveler

scraped off his or her pots along the stream bank is unappetizing when you go to fill your pots to boil cooking water. Don't rationalize cleaning dishes as "just feeding the fish." Take the extra precautions. Keep the streams clean.

Purifying Water

Almost all backcountry water is now polluted with *Giardia lamblia* and bacteria. To avoid the very unpleasant consequences of ingesting these tiny devils, be sure to boil all water (to a rolling boil), filter the water through a carbon filter, or treat every quart with two or three drops of iodine (wait thirty minutes

The best way to take a bath in the backcountry is to do so far from any natural source of water.

Above: In Colorado, as in most places in the United States, free-running water is no longer safe to drink. Horses, however, seem to be immune to the water-borne bugs that plague humans. I use discretion about when and where I let my horses drink, but up in the high country they seem to be okay. Below: My friend Mike cooks dinner on an ultralight backpacking stove after a day on the trail. My dog, Nicky, is too tired even to notice there is food being prepared.

before ingesting). Backpacking filters are great, provided that you follow the instructions carefully and don't get your filtered water contaminated. Speaking from firsthand experience, I can tell you that diarrhea is not compatible with high-quality horseback riding. It's definitely better to be safe than sorry!

Another wise practice is to always wash your hands with a little bleach before you handle food or begin cooking. Hand-transferred fecal contamination is a real cause of concern in backcountry cooking. Hygiene is important! Rinsing your dishes in a bleach solution before you put them away helps, too.

Fires

On the subject of cooking: In this day and age, with more and more people wanting to use less and less wilderness, fires should be used only for emergencies. All cooking should be done on gas stoves. If you feel you must have a campfire, reserve it for a special night, and keep it small. Here are some tips.

• Gather firewood far away from camp (most campsites are already stripped of dead wood as high as you can reach, by previous campers).

• Spread out your wood gathering so that it is not noticeable, and use as little as possible.

• Prepare the fireside by removing the top layers of soil, down to mineral soil.

• Do not keep the fire going all night.

• Burn all firewood down to white ash.

• Before departing, when you are absolutely sure the fire is dead out, carefully replace the soil you removed.

I have each rider bring a miner's candle. With these all lit and placed in a small circle they make a passable substitute for a campfire.

With everything you do, remember, this is a fragile environment. It needs our thoughtful care to survive in its natural state. Not only is it a pleasing thought that someone else might enjoy finding it intact as you did, but you might even come this way again yourself someday.

CHAPTER THREE

Adventures on Horseback

HORSES AND COURAGE

hen Diane called me and we started planning her family's custom-designed riding vacation, I had a feeling that her family was special. It wasn't until I met them in person, however, that I realized just how special they really were. Diane and her husband, Lonnie, wanted to spend a week in Colorado with one of their two sons, Nick. In our first phone conversation I learned that Nick was twenty-one and had a slight disability that caused a balance problem. He had already done some riding at a summer camp, and Diane had confidence that he could handle more.

A few days later, sitting around camp and sipping hot chocolate after the chores had been completed, I heard more of the story. Nick had been born hydrocephalic. He had water on the brain. The most obvious outward effect of this condition is a head that is proportionately larger than most people's heads. The pressure inside his head affected, among other things, his hearing and balance.

The doctors' prognosis had been bleak. Severe retardation, blindness, and most likely death within the first year were the predictions. Twenty-one years later, Nick was finishing his second year of college. Nick, Lonnie, and Diane were living proof of a belief that is commonplace among the disabled community: Never underestimate human determination or the ability to adapt.

It was Nick's love of horses that inspired his family to go on a low-impact horse camping trip with me. Below: Nick and I put the bridle on Chapa.

It was Nick's love of horses, along with a desire to strengthen family ties, that had brought these "city slickers" out to Colorado to go on one of my Conquistador Rides. It had been Nick's choice! It seemed like a logical choice to them to use my Peruvian Paso horses with their smooth gait to compensate for Nick's balance problem. I guess I could have refused the challenge or used insurance issues or the dangers of mountain trail riding as an excuse to politely say no, but I felt there was something larger at stake here. Besides, this family had years of experience canoe camping and were already familiar with the requirements of low-impact camping. In addition, our conquistador ride program at West's Peruvian Paso Center had been founded on the idea of providing clients with safe but challenging outdoor learning experiences.

On that first day of our trip, I realized that Nick was going to need some extra assistance. Chapa, his riding horse, had become more and more irritated as Nick's excitement flowed from his hands through the reins and into the bit. I took the bridle off Chapa and gave it to Nick to look at. When he held the bit in his two hands and I handled the reins, he was able to feel the difference between heavy hands and light hands. That way he could experience what Chapa had been feeling as Nick was riding him.

The lesson worked. Nick softened his touch and Chapa relaxed in response. Soon they were just two good buddies, enjoying each other's company.

After a few days of arena work and short trail rides, we were ready to ride into our first campsite. I was in the lead,

There was a brief moment of eerie stillness before the wind hit with hurricane force.

scouting the trail with the others strung out behind me. After climbing one particularly steep part of the trail, I turned in my saddle and looked back down the trail, checking to see how my three clients were doing. I was just in time to see a menacing black cloud, rolling over itself like some crazy misplaced ocean wave, roaring up the narrow mountain valley. Even as I yelled to everyone to get down and pull on their rain gear, I scrambled to take my own advice. There was a brief moment of eerie stillness before the wind hit with full hurricane force. The thunder was almost deafening as lightning struck high points on the ridges all around us.

Behind the wall of wind came a sheet of rain, soaking everything in its path, including us. We struggled to get into slickers and keep control of the frightened horses. By the time the storm's fury had passed over us, we were already shivering from the wet and cold. No one voiced any objection when I suggested that we turn around and head back down, toward our camp.

We decided to descend on foot for a while, leading the horses, hoping the effort would bring some warmth back into numb fingers and toes. It was still raining. We didn't have to go far to see the dramatic effect the storm had wreaked on a nearby aspen grove. Huge trees, standing only moments earlier, were now laid down topsy-turvy, some completely blocking the trail. Nothing was said, but I knew that everyone realized how lucky we had been. One of these giants could have come crashing down on us! Navigating the obstructed trail presented a tedious challenge. I gained a new appreciation and respect for the stamina and determination

Nick and his family saddle up for a backcountry adventure.

of the early mountain men who had first explored this rugged country without trails.

The rain slowed to a steady drizzle. We mounted our horses and rode. As we traversed lower down into the valley, the trail changed from rough and rocky to slick and slimy. On the steeper slopes, the horses locked their hind legs and slid down, leaving six-foot-long skid marks in the gooey clay soil. It was amazing how they were able to keep their balance and maintain their footing under such difficult conditions. Still, I secretly held my breath with concern for the safety of my riders, even as I marveled at the sure-footed abilities of these Peruvian Paso horses.

The trail dropped into the valley bottom, crossed the creek, and wound around a steep side hill. As we came out of an aspen grove, it turned sharply to the right and went almost straight up. Above us, we could see the low saddle that divided this drainage from the one we were camped in. The trail leading to it looked like a toboggan slide, filled with mud. The horses tackled the new challenge willingly enough. They would lunge forward, three or four steps at a time, then stop to catch their breath. With muscles straining to keep their balance, they would slide backward, losing most of the ground they had gained.

By now their sides were heaving, and they were quivering from the strain. Sure that at any moment one of them would go down, with a rider underneath, I called a halt to this "rodeo." We dismounted, tied up the reins, and turned the horses loose to scramble up on their own. The mud was so slick that it was almost impossible to stand, let alone walk up the hill. Using scrub oak for handholds, Diane and Nick started to work their way off to the side of the trail. They were clinging to each other, as well as any handy branches they could grab for support.

Lonnie and I were able to pull ourselves up, hand over hand. Reaching the top, breathless and covered with mud, we secured two of the horses. The others we just let go. I knew they wouldn't stray far from their buddies. I started back down to help Diane and Nick. In a flash, I was sliding out of control, first on my feet, and then on the seat of my jeans. By the time I reached them, I was a muddy mess. This kind of humiliation isn't supposed to happen to the guide! We all got a good belly laugh out of my predicament. That helped relieve the tension.

With a lot of mutual assistance, we all made it to the top, scraped off the mud, and remounted the horses. When we finally reached our camp near the valley floor, we were all greatly relieved and exhilarated. We were in awe of the fantastic horses that had carried us and shared our adventure. Smiles and

Once again, I was reminded that the candle of life burns brightest in the winds of adventure.

congratulations were exchanged all around. Everyone agreed that we now shared the spirit of the *conquistadors* who had ridden through this country long ago.

That night, the routine of camp chores was something of a celebration. As we worked together to care for the horses and cook our meal, I felt proud of my students.

On our last day together, we trailered the horses out to Rabbit Valley, on the Colorado-Utah border. This is slick rock country; beautiful desert canyons filled with windblown sand, wild flowers, piñon and juniper, humbled by towering cliffs and spires of desert sandstone. We went early in the morning to beat the heat of the day. The horses were full of energy. Miles fell behind easily. We were captured by the never-ending kaleidoscope of desert beauty, constantly rearranging itself in front of our eyes. From time to time we reined in and just sat still, soaking up the scenery. From every knoll you could take in the beauty, the quiet, and the empty country surrounding us in all directions.

Something had happened. We were no longer just clients and guide. We were four friends sharing this experience together. The adventure was nearly over, but the friendship and memories would go on.

The fact that Nick had been born with some physical and mental challenges hadn't stood in the way of his accomplishment. The dream of an adventure on horseback had been Nick's idea. The courage to take action, to pursue that dream, was Nick's choice. I had shared the adventure and been enriched by it. Once again, I was reminded that the candle of life burns brightest in the winds of adventure. Nick's candle burned brightly on his Conquistador Ride. I am able to see a little more clearly because of that light. 🐎

SLEEPING WELL OUT ON THE TRAIL

As you evaluate your equipment for low-impact horse camping, you need to consider three things: weight, compressibility, and versatility. What camping gear weighs the least, takes up the least space, and gives the widest range of comfort? Trust me, it's not a cowboy bedroll.

What you need are a good tent, a sleeping bag, and a foam pad.

A Quality Tent

With a quality nylon-back-packing tent, you can get out of the elements quickly when the weather turns nasty on you. The tent should accommodate two people, and have a waterproof fly and floor to keep you dry, plus breathable walls to wick away body moisture and cut down air currents. It should be big enough to let you move around inside without always touching the walls, but not so big that your body warmth can't heat up the interior. That way, you can be warm and dry inside, sipping tea in your long johns while the wind and rain trash the world outside at five degrees below freezing. The tent, fly, and poles should weigh about 4½ to 6 pounds. That means your total weight per person for this two-person tent is about 2 ½ pounds.

A Lightweight Sleeping Bag

A good tent also allows you to get by with a lighter-weight sleeping bag. You do not need a winter-expedition-weight bag. Usually, a three-season bag, weighing about 2½ to 3 pounds, is all you need. Personally, I prefer the freedom of movement I get in a semirectangular bag to that of a full mummy bag. I can regulate my body temperature easier and be just as warm by pulling on more clothes if I need them to sleep. But, I can get a better night's sleep if I'm able to move my legs around independent of each other. It's a personal choice.

A Sleeping Pad

The other very important item needed for a good night's rest is a sleeping pad. A three-quarter-length, self-inflating air mattress works great. They weigh about 1½ pounds and are perfect for rolling your tent poles into while traveling. With an extra little kit, they quickly convert to a handy camp chair. Just like being at the beach!

Comfort and Security

Naturally, these items don't come cheap. If you want quality, you have to pay for it. But with careful selection and a reasonably well-padded pocketbook, you can get your sleeping and living accommodations down to about 6 to 7 pounds per person. You will have very little bulk and can ensure a reasonable level of comfort and security under even the worst circumstances.

CAMPING COWBOY-STYLE

When looking through the popular Western horse magazines these days, it's easy to see that we are going through another period of cowboy nostalgia: a longing for our more comprehensible and colorful past.

It's worth noting, however, that the classic period we cherish and celebrate with such gusto today was, in fact, a fleeting moment in history, a flash in the pan that began with the near extermination of the buffalo and ended with the invention of barbed wire. Still, that short period has come to symbolize a time of freedom and adventure, when men were men and a man was judged by his ability to ride, rope, and shoot. Back then, a handshake sealed a deal, and you could count on a man to be as good as his word. Oh, the good old days!

How good those good old days really were for the men and women who were actually trying to eke out a living in them is a matter for speculation. However, one thing is for sure.

The cowboy was a pragmatist. He appreciated things that worked. That's why the lever-action saddle rifle and the six-shooter replaced the single-shot muzzleloader and sword, almost overnight. I have no doubt that he would have embraced many of the things that our modern technology has made available to us, even if he questioned the values that support that technology. In short, I think the horseman of old appreciated his creature comforts and did everything possible to accommodate them. His gear reflected his needs. If there had been something better, he would have taken advantage of it.

So I have to smile when I see ads for such items as the cowboy bedroll. Sleeping out under the stars, wrapped up in your heavy canvas bedroll and wool blankets, is a romantic idea. That is, as long as you aren't too far from the pickup truck so you can crawl in and turn on the heater if it starts to rain or the temperature takes a tumble. For someone who is serious about wilderness horse travel, bedrolls make about as much sense as a bikini on an Eskimo.

When selecting your gear for a low-impact horse camping trip, just keep in mind my slogan, Go right – go light.

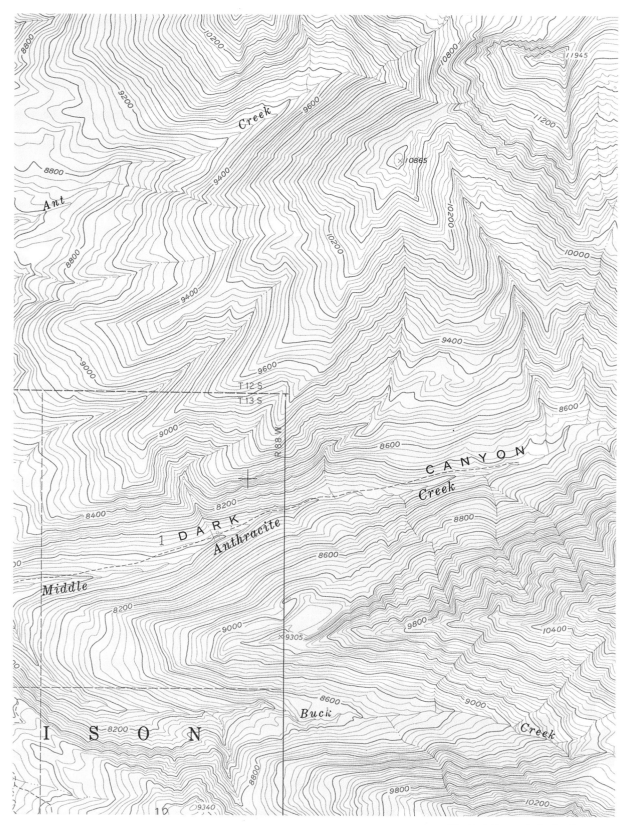

The Dark Canyon is flanked by mountain ranges soaring above 10,000 feet.

The Dark Canyon Ride

Most people have dreams and fantasies. Some lucky people even get to act out some of their fantasies. But to be living a fantasy and to be able to savor its essence, as though you were watching a movie in which you are the hero and star — now that's an unusual and special event. I had just been having one of those rare, memorable moments when the ground literally fell out from under my horse's feet. Without warning, I was thrown into a life-or-death situation that I would only come to appreciate much later.

Each year, at the height of the fall color season in late September, I would pack my gear and take off for a week of solitude in the mountains of western Colorado: just me, my dog Nicky and, of course, my horse. Although I had been doing this for many years, the spirit of high adventure never failed to stir within me as I gathered up my gear and pored over topographic (topo) maps, trying to come up with a general plan of where my wanderings would take me. This year I decided to ride right from my ranch across the Forest Service land and into the West Elk Wilderness. My destination was the Dark Canyon. The map showed a trail going down into the canyon on the south side, but there was nothing shown ascending to the top, to the north, to meet up with a main trail, a mile or so above. I'd just have to figure it out when I got there.

I rode my Peruvian Paso stallion Carmel. I had been riding and camping for three days without running into a soul. The trail to the edge of the Dark Canyon, so easy looking on the topo map, had deteriorated into a little-used and almost indistinguishable path through a sea of aspens. Although I was having some trouble finding a route, I wasn't too concerned. I was deep in rapture, enjoying the changing colors of the aspens and willows and the fresh, crisp smell of the mountain air on this magnificent fall day.

The smell of wood smoke, wafting through the dense grove of aspen trees, snapped me out of my daydream. It seemed like all three of us — the dog, the horse, and I — became aware of this intrusion into our separate private worlds at exactly the same moment. With Nicky barking and my horse whinnying and prancing, we headed off to the west, through an open meadow toward a small, white sheepherder's wall tent. As I rode nearer, the smell of coffee brewing and bread baking mingled with the aspen smoke. I could feel the juices go to work in my stomach, already anticipating a tasty midafternoon snack.

As I sat there taking in the scene, the tent flap was suddenly thrown back. A short man with dark features and a big black mustache was smiling at me. In his hand was one of those blue enameled-metal cups, filled with steaming coffee. It was just like something out of a cowboy movie. He invited me to step down. In no time we were old friends, laughing and smiling and getting along famously with my high school Spanish and his broken English. I enjoyed some of the best coffee and fresh-baked sourdough bread that I'd ever had. He seemed happy to have some company. Feeling very satisfied and full of life, I said *"Adios"* to my newfound *amigo,* mounted up again, and headed off to meet my destiny, leaving him to his sheep and his solitude.

I soon picked up the trail again. A half hour's ride found me coming out along the edge of the aspens, looking down into the Dark Canyon. Now this isn't a big canyon as canyons go. It is nothing on the scale of the Grand Canyon or the Branca del Cobre in Mexico. The beauty of this canyon is its darkness, its remoteness, and its feeling of loneliness. As I rode along the rim, looking for the trail, it was easy to see why it had been so named. Its sides were not vertical, but they were plenty steep. Growing on the many ledges below were thick stands of spruce and fir, giving the place a very dark look.

Suddenly, the ground under Carmel's hooves gave way. In a split second we were falling, tumbling end over end!

The canyon had been cut by a stream between two mountains. The walls seemed too close together, as though a single mountain had been split in two. This close proximity cut off the sunlight and added to the canyon's somber, almost sinister, appearance.

The wind was blowing up out of the bottom. At times, it brought sounds of the running stream far below. Maybe it was the mood I was in, but it sounded strangely like voices whispering my name. That dramatically heightened the spot's lonely, desolate, almost forboding feeling.

We drifted along the edge, occasionally looking here and there over the lip to see if the trail was evident anywhere below. It looked as though the trail had made its way over the edge at a certain spot years ago, but erosion had washed the lip away. Now there was just a sheer drop-off. Even so, I wasn't too concerned, yet. I wasn't in a hurry. Eventually I'd find a way down. And besides, I was still enjoying the taste of coffee on my tongue and contemplating the wonder of life's mysteries.

Suddenly, the ground under Carmel's hooves gave way. In a split second we were falling, tumbling end over end!

The initial fall wasn't that far, maybe five feet or so. But the canyon's side remained very steep for another hundred feet below. At first it was all I could do to keep from getting crushed under my horse. Carmel kept falling, then trying to get his feet under him, only to roll over sideways again. After his first few rolls, I managed to get free of him. I just slid down the embankment on the seat of my jeans, watching in horror as he got his footing, looked straight up the hill at me, and then tumbled backward, rolling over and over and over. When he finally came to a stop, he was standing on all four legs, but they were held stiff, sticking out at crazy angles. He looked like a sawhorse. He was staring straight up the hill, his eyes as big as saucers. He just stood there, motionless. As I came down to him, I realized that he was shaking all over. He was in shock! And then I realized, so was I!

Carmel had blood running out of numerous scrapes and cuts in various places where his hide had come off. It looked as if he had blood coming out of his ears, too. I thought to myself, Oh no!

He's fractured his skull. A closer look brought some relief. The blood was coming from cuts on his ears and forehead. I immediately stripped off his gear and saddle. I took my time checking him. I went over him carefully, palpating for injuries. Amazingly, nothing seemed to be broken. Somehow, even the saddle and all my gear was in one piece. As I repacked, I looked back up to the crest of the canyon and realized how lucky we were to still be alive. I said a brief thank you to the Great Spirit.

I also realized that we were trapped, or at least there was no visible exit from this place the way we had come in. Leading Carmel, I started downhill, carefully picking my way toward the bottom. We were both still very shaky. It was getting dark. I had to find a place to camp near water.

Life

Life is not a prize to win
Life is just
a game to play
Youre not rewarded
in the end
You have to live it
day by day

Don't sit and fret
about the past
Or worry 'bout what's
yet to come
Just focus on
the present day
Keep on your path
and have some fun

— Don West

WHEN I FINALLY did get my little tent set up, it was in a grassy meadow just above the stream. I bathed Carmel's injuries in the cold water of the stream and then tied up the night high line for him. In a nearby tree I noticed a big river rock, the size of a man's head, staring at me from between the branches . . . at eye level! We were obviously in an area of flash floods. The rock in the tree showed just how high the water could get and how powerful it could be.

As complete darkness fell over the canyon, I listened to the lonely wail of coyotes off in the distance. I watched with fascination as a lone cow elk seemed to appear out of nowhere and picked her way carefully along the opposite shore of the stream. In spite of everything, or perhaps because of it, I felt unusually happy. That night I slept soundly.

The next morning I awoke with a start. It wasn't the sound of rushing water that brought me abruptly out of my deep sleep, as I had imagined the night before. No, it was the dead silence! I lay there, motionless, holding my breath. I listened. In the early morning light, shadows around me began to take shape. But there was no sound. Where was the expected occasional tinkling of Carmel's night bell?

Instant panic grabbed my throat. A cold sweat broke out all over my body. I immediately jumped up and pulled on my shoes. A quick search of the area confirmed my worst fears. Somehow, Carmel had gotten the gate on the carabiner open and had freed himself from the long stakeout high line. I searched the ground for hoofprints. It was easy to see where a hobbled horse had started up out of the canyon.

As my joy gave way to less noble emotions, I realized how frightened I had been. This certainly was no place to lose your horse!

Let me tell you, a horse that has learned how to handle hobbles can cover a lot of ground in the course of a night. A fifteen-minute climb finally brought the faint sound of a ringing bell off in the distance. I can't begin to describe to you the sense of relief I felt. Another few minutes brought Carmel into sight, contentedly munching grass in the middle of an old, dried-out beaver pond. A series of ancient dams had filled up with silt, becoming tiny, grassy meadows.

As my joy gave way to less noble emotions, I realized how frightened I had been. This certainly was no place to lose your damn horse! Once again, I felt very lucky. Things could have turned out much worse. Once again I thanked the Great Spirit for letting me off the hook. As I led Carmel back to my little camp, I felt relieved and contrite. I made my morning coffee and oatmeal, and hummed a little tune. I felt happy.

Savoring my second cup of coffee, I took a good long look at the map. If I crossed the stream, there might be a way up through the dark timber and aspen groves that alternated dominating the steep ledges and benches above. It looked impenetrable and very uninviting. In fact, a solid wall of dark timber stood right at the stream's edge. I couldn't even see any obvious place to get started. My alternative was to go downstream, into the canyon between the mountains. According to my topo map, there was a considerable altitude drop in a short distance. In about a mile this stream, the Ruby Anthracite Creek, joined Anthracite Creek and flowed west around Marcellina Mountain. Paralleling that second stream was a well-used pack trail that climbed the Devil's Stairway and circled back around, high above my present camp. I chose what appeared to be the path of least resistance, the shorter route. I packed up and headed on downstream.

At first I stayed on the stream's south side. It turned out to be a good decision. I hadn't gone far, maybe a few hundred yards, before the embankment on the other side turned into a vertical rock cliff that shot right out of the water. It towered over my head. At the same time, on my side of the stream, the ground became steeper and rockier, pushing me closer and

I slid off, into the icy water, and let Carmel pull me along.

closer to the water's edge. I tried to stay out of the stream, leading Carmel through a minefield of big flat boulders. As these rock plates became larger and closer together, they got more and more unstable, developing into what is known as a talus slope. The talus extended up the mountain as far as I could see, and right down into the water.

Finally I felt that this was just too tedious, and too dangerous for Carmel. He was nervous, sensing the danger, as large blocks of rock moved precariously under his hooves, but brave soul that he is, he was picking his way carefully and steadily along. Many of the big slabs were so unstable that they actually seesawed under his weight. It was nerve-racking, for both of us.

I had no choice. I opted for the stream. Carmel seemed relieved. He went into the water willingly. Now we were making good time. At first it was easy going. We would go about a hundred feet then cross a rock bank that would form a small pool below us. Each successive rock bank became slightly bigger. Each pool became bigger, too! Soon the pools were too deep to walk through. Carmel was forced to swim. I just slid off, into the icy water, held on to the saddle, and let him pull me along. By now, we had worked our way into a place where the two mountains came very close together. Looking ahead, as far as I could see, there was nothing but rock and water: just a series of crystal clear pools, locked between rock cliffs and divided by small waterfalls.

I felt sure we had come more than halfway. It couldn't be more than half a mile to the river junction and the trail. We pushed on. There was no way to get out of the water on either side now. Carmel had to scramble onto the edge of the dividing rock dikes, then jump into the pool below. I could see that the drops into the succeeding pools became higher. Even if Carmel had been willing to do it, I was afraid that he would land on something sharp and impale himself. Or, an equally disconcerting thought, we might get trapped below, and not be able to go in either direction. The vision of having my horse stuck in this lonely and forbidding place was very sobering.

I weighed the choices and made my decision. With one long last look down that deep dark stretch of canyon, we turned and started tediously retracing our steps, back the way we had come. Now at least I knew why there was no trail through this part of the Dark Canyon!

The first few pools proved to be very difficult for Carmel to climb out of. He would wade and swim through the pools, but he had trouble getting any footing on the steep walls at the end. A couple of times he almost managed to scramble up, when his shoes lost their grip and he fell, smashing his knees and chin on the protruding rocks. This made him very nervous. It was obvious that he, too, knew we were in trouble. He began to sweat and shake in spite of the cold temperatures. I was doing my share of shivering, too. It became clear that we both had had enough adventure for one day. Finally we were out of the steep stretch.

ALPENGLOW STARTED to spread over the peaks as once again I set up my little tent, in the same place we had camped the night before. This time I used two carabiners with their gates reversed to make sure Carmel wasn't going anywhere during the night. I built a small fire, something I rarely do, to warm my bones . . . and lift my spirit. Although I was exhausted, I stayed up very late that night, throwing a few sticks on my fire and watching Orion chase Taurus the Bull, who was chasing the Seven Sisters across the heavens. I wondered how many other generations of horsemen had lived through some similar adventure and savored the eternal wonder of life while staring into the flames of a warming campfire.

The next morning I broke camp quickly. During the night the weather had warmed up, a sure sign of a new front coming in bringing a change in the weather. The smell of impending snow hung in the air. I didn't want to be snowed-in in this canyon any more than I wanted to be drowned in it. Then I remembered the cow elk I had seen two nights before. How had she found her way down to the stream? I crossed at a narrow place to have a look.

A little scouting around brought good results. I picked up a cleverly concealed elk trail that was obviously well used. A few hours of fairly easy going brought me to the canyon's north rim, where my path joined the main trail. It was only a little track through the wilderness, just wide enough for one horse — but right then it looked like a superhighway!

That night, in a high mountain meadow tucked into a cluster of giant blue spruce and Douglas fir, secluded among the larger grove of aspen trees, I watched the snow drift down and reflected on the past few days. At times the outcome had been uncertain. On occasion, my life and the life of my horse had been in jeopardy. A few times, we narrowly escaped dire consequences. Isn't it interesting that those moments stood out most vividly in my memory as the times when I felt most alive? I sensed that Carmel and Nicky felt the same way, too. I realized, once again, that the mountains speak the loudest to those who pay with sweat to hear their voices.

As I sat cross-legged in front of my tiny tent, sipping my last cup of coffee, I listened contentedly to the voice of the mountains. The silence was music to my ears, and the solitude was food for my soul.

RIDE SOME, REST SOME

If you dismount and walk up or down steep sections of the trail, it is good for your horse and good for you. It saves both of you, gives you a little exercise, and makes it possible to cover more miles in a day.

Steep downhills are really the toughest on horses, especially young ones who are still growing and laying down bone. Walking alongside your horse as you go down a steep hill is a good time to check your crupper, making sure it's tight enough to do its job.

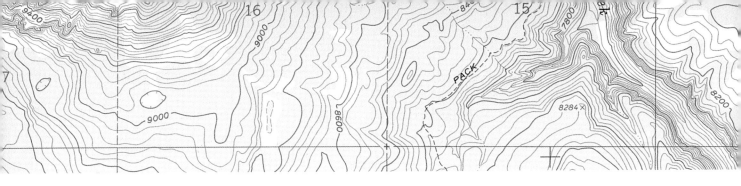

CHAPTER FOUR

Life Is a Trail

HUNTING BARE

t was a beautiful, sunshiny day. We'd already had a week of Indian summer, with crisp, cold mornings that made the fallen, frozen aspen leaves crunch softly underfoot. I saddled my horse, packed up my gear, and set off for my annual elk hunt.

I had been planning the outing for some time, impatiently looking forward to exchanging the ranch routine for the mountains' solitude. As I went through my checklist, I felt relaxed and confident. I had gone over my equipment a couple of times, just to be sure I hadn't left anything out or packed something I didn't need. I was confident of a pleasurable experience, even if I didn't shoot an elk. I knew the country I was going into quite well. Over the summer I had taken many day rides there, conditioning the horses and getting a feel for the area.

I had already located the perfect spot for my camp. It was in a stand of black timber along the edge of a twenty-acre (roughly rectangular) open park situated high up on the mountainside. A nameless little stream meandered through the middle, giving easy access to water. There was plenty of good grass for the horse and dead, dry wood for my fire. A small hill, located just to the west of the camp, would provide good wind protection should one of those hard-blowing, early fall storms come in.

It was like a dream, riding into camp that afternoon. Carmel was feeling good. My mind was just as free and easy as the stallion's four-beat Paso gait.

By checking my topo map, I figured the camp to be at about 10,000 feet, only 1,000 feet or so below timberline. The 13,000-foot peaks, wearing a new garment of snow, towered above.

I loaded Carmel into the trailer and drove to the trailhead, where I left my rig. At the time, Carmel was only three years old. This was his first year under saddle. He was already a veteran of many short training rides, including a couple of easy overnight trips into the backcountry, but this was his first solo ride. He would be out all alone, with no horse buddies to reassure him and keep him company.

I wasn't taking a packhorse. I had laid out my kit carefully to be sure I wasn't packing any extra items. I had just what I needed for a comfortable, albeit Spartan, four-day solo camp. Everything fit neatly into my own system of saddle bags and cantle bag. They fit tightly behind my cantle and curved around neatly behind my legs. My hobbles were buckled around my horse's neck. My rifle hung down the left side, counterbalanced on the off side by the night rope, water bottles, and horse feed in my pommel bags. Carmel wore his halter, lead rope, and bosal, completing my outfit.

It was like a dream, riding into camp that afternoon. Carmel was feeling good. My mind was just as free and easy as the stallion's four-beat Paso gait. Most of the leaves had fallen from the trees by now, casualties of the fall's early light freezes. They lay scattered like a rich, rusty carpet all over the forest floor. Their demise had opened up many new vistas through the aspens, previously blocked by the thick green foliage of summer. The diffused light filtering through the bare tree branches made me feel as if I were a samurai warrior riding through a Japanese painting.

Although it was about a seven-mile pull up into camp, with a 2,500-foot gain in altitude, we made it without working up much of a sweat. To save Carmel at his tender age, I stepped down and walked up the steep sections of the trail. Truth is, this has always been my habit: to stretch my legs on the ups and downs and let the horse carry me over the easier country.

Although there had been a few truck and trailer outfits at the trailhead, I hadn't seen another person all the way in. I wondered if there would be any other hunters camped up around "my park." As I came across the last little rise and looked out over the high mountain meadow, I was pleased to find that I had it all to myself, at least for the first night. I knew that the morning would undoubtedly bring hunters, making their way up from the lower country, probably pushing little bunches of elk up in front of them. Things would hopefully get busy for me then. But for now, the entire wilderness area was mine to enjoy alone.

I untied my saddlebags, stripped the saddle and bosal off Carmel, and started looking for just the right place to put up my tent. I had about an hour before dark, just enough time to get camp set up and eat dinner before I ran out of light. Already there was a sharp chill in the air. I figured it would be a crystal clear night. I pulled on my vest and jacket and did a little dance, just to get my blood going. It took me only a few minutes to find a place flat and long enough for my little tent. It snuggled in perfectly between two big spruce trees. It was easy to put up. Once I had the fly tightly fastened down, I threw my things inside. *Voilà!* Instant home! I covered my saddle with a plastic garbage bag, and my camp was complete.

I fixed supper almost as quickly. Although I still indulge myself by making a small campfire on some special evenings just for the cheeriness of it, I do all of my cooking over a mini-backpacking stove. It's much cleaner and more efficient and makes it easier to leave the camp looking unspoiled. That's the way I like people to leave camps for me, too. Cooking fires tend to leave permanent scars, use up a lot of firewood (detracting from the wilderness quality of the area), and are hard to hide. My supper was a one-pot affair; sort of a mulligan stew, high on the carbs, with tuna, noodles, cheese, and some peas all mixed together. Dehydrated applesauce, washed down with plenty of coffee, and a shot of apricot brandy finished off the affair.

With my stomach full, it was time to stake Carmel out for the night. After he had taken a good drink, I took him into the middle of the meadow, where the grass looked thickest. There were no trees high enough for the night rope, so I found a big old dead snag to tie Carmel up to. It was heavy enough so he couldn't pull it around.

Next I put the hobbles on, around the pasterns of Carmel's front legs. While you are sleeping, remember, your horse will be moving around, eating. The last thing I did before saying goodnight to Carmel was to put on his bell.

Carmel happily rests in this grassy meadow.

By the time I finished with Carmel, the first stars twinkled in a crystal clear sky. The darkness settled in as though a giant black blanket had been gently folded around the mountains, tucking them in for the night. I made my way back to my little stand of trees and got down into the cocoonlike nest of my tent and sleeping bag. I wiggled in, zipped up, and was asleep in no time at all.

It was the heat that woke me up. As I slid back into the world of consciousness, I realized that I was hot and sweaty in my polypropylene long johns. Then I noticed that everything was very quiet.

I peeked out of the tent. Much to my surprise, the world had been transformed to white by an early winter snowstorm. The air was still and warm. Giant flakes were falling from the sky like gossamer ghosts. I wormed out of my underwear; that felt a little more comfortable! As I lay in my unzipped bag, I thought about the good tracking I'd have in the skim of fresh snow come morning. Half daydreaming, I heard Carmel's bell out in the meadow. It sounded like he'd gotten himself tangled up and was trying to get loose. I figured that checking on him would be a good excuse to get out of the tent and cool off.

Hobbles won't keep a horse from getting away, since horses quickly learn to travel in them. But they will slow a horse down and keep him from getting seriously hurt if he runs hard to the end of the picket rope.

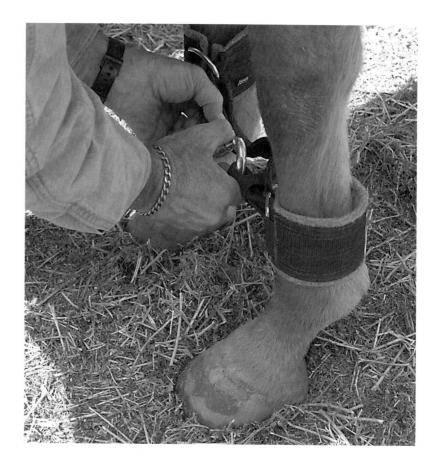

Good hobbles should be soft and at least two inches wide. You don't want a sore-legged horse come morning.

The darkness settled in as though a giant black blanket had been gently folded around the mountains, tucking them in for the night.

I pulled on my socks, boots, and hat, grabbed my headlamp, and headed out to have a look. The snow felt refreshingly cool as it melted almost instantly on my hot bare skin. I couldn't see more than ten feet in any direction, but I didn't have any trouble going toward the sound of the ringing bell. Then, suddenly, the bell stopped. I stopped, too, and listened. I went ahead, to where I thought Carmel must be, but I couldn't find him. By now, I was getting plenty wet, and a little cold, too. When I left my tent, I thought this expedition would only take a couple of minutes. But now, I was starting to get a little uncomfortable — and a little concerned.

Right then, I heard the bell. It was off to my right. Much to my surprise, Carmel was only about twenty feet away from me! It was snowing harder now. The falling snow muffled the sound and cut down the visibility. I couldn't see him even at that short distance. He wasn't moving, and no wonder. He had totally wrapped his rope around the snag and was held tight, with his head just inches above the ground. It took only a minute or two to free him and get his rope untangled, but by then I was really getting cold. I started shivering uncontrollably. My teeth were chattering, and my fingers were beginning to get numb.

That's when the bad news sank in. In my efforts to free Carmel I had lost all sense of direction. I had no idea how to get back to my tent. A rush of fear ran up my spine. I looked around with my flashlight, trying to sort out my tracks. Damn! In the process of untangling Carmel's rope, I had made tracks in all directions. The snow was coming down hard, quickly covering my old tracks. Visibility was almost zero. I realized I'd never find the right set of tracks leading back to my tent. I was, as they say, in deep — er — trouble!

I decided to trust my intuition, go straight ahead in any old direction, and see if I would just get lucky. I went out fast, about fifty yards, looked around, then headed back. I thought I had a pretty fair idea how far it should be to my little stand of trees. I went out only that far and then quickly followed my tracks back to Carmel. Now, of course, I could find him by the sound

In my efforts to free Carmel I had lost all sense of direction. I had no idea how to get back to my tent! A rush of fear ran up my spine.

of his bell. It made a steady ringing as he raised and lowered his head, placidly eating, unconcerned about my naked plight as I shivered and froze to death!

After three or four unsuccessful attempts, I really started to feel concerned. Even so, I had to laugh at myself, imagining how I must look. I pictured how the obituary might read: "Naked man wearing just his hat and boots found frozen to death near horse." The headline would leave a lot of room for humorous speculation.

On my next try, I went a little farther and found a stand of trees but no camp. I ran back and forth along the timber's edge between the trees and the meadow. Just as I was about to give up and head back to Carmel, my light caught the outline of my tent. What a relief! A moment later I was pulling on my dry long underwear and firing up the stove for a cup of hot soup.

I didn't stop shaking for hours. I didn't go out to check on Carmel again that night, either.

The next morning I was up early. I made a breakfast of hot cereal, eggs, bacon, hot Tang, and plenty of coffee. Food never tasted so good! It was still snowing lightly. I didn't venture far from camp. I moved Carmel to a new location and tied him to a high line. He seemed content to work on a little patch of fresh grass. I walked a hundred yards or so to the edge of the small hill. I curled up under a lone bull spruce tree with a good view of the open country below.

Sure enough, some approaching hunters pushed a big bull elk right by my stand for an easy, clean kill. Two more bulls, both lung-shot and blowing bubbles of blood, came staggering up the hill. The hunters, who had wounded them down below, were happy to claim their trophies without having to track and possibly lose their prey.

As I skinned and dressed the elk, the skies cleared and the sun shone brightly. The day warmed. By the time I had Carmel packed with two quarters of the elk and the other quarters pulled high into a tree, the snow was gone and the ground was bare again. I caught myself humming a little tune, feeling very lucky to be alive. My expedition had been a success. I'd survived another mini-adventure and learned a few good lessons in the process. 🐎

My bosal hangs out to dry in a nearby tree.

TYING UP YOUR HORSE

Remember the little saying about trusting in Allah but tying up your camel? Well, it's also important to be able to untie him when you want to. A camel, or a horse, tied up in a way that makes it hard (or impossible) to untie him in an emergency is an accident waiting to happen, especially when the horse is applying full force on the other end. It is best to learn how to tie up correctly right at the start, and then make it a permanent habit. Remember, repetition is the mother of skill. Practice makes perfect. So learn to tie up your horse right, right now, and avoid an unnecessary FUBAR (fouled up beyond any repair) in the future.

1. Holding the working end of the lead rope (the part that goes to the horse) with your right hand, use your left hand to throw the loose end of the rope over the top of the rail you're going to tie to. Grab the loose end from underneath with your left hand.

2. Holding your hands 16 to 24 inches below the rail, adjust the rope length so that the horse has enough slack in the working end but can't step over the rope or get caught in it.

3. Make a loop with the rope in your left hand, bringing the loose end around the front of the rope from right to left.

4. Bring the loose end around the back of the loop and around the working end of the rope (the part that goes to the horse).

5. Double the loose end and push it down through the loop in your left hand. Pull the knot tight to form a figure eight.

6. The loose end will still be hanging free. To secure your horse when you are not there, run the loose end through the new loop you have just created. this will prevent the horse from untying the knot by pulling on the rope.

7. To untie, pull the loose end. If the knot is properly tied it will pull free, even under pressure.

Always try to tie your horse high. A frightened horse who pulls back with full force can get more leverage and do more damage (possibly to himself) if he is tied low.

My Annual Elk Hunt

My annual elk hunt was, by choice, a solo affair. I always looked forward to it with quiet enthusiasm. For me, it was a contemplative time of special significance. I don't want to get mired down in mushy sentimentality here, but the hunting (and the kill) of a magnificent creature that I have great respect and admiration for has always had serious spiritual significance for me. My hunt was definitely not a trophy hunt. It was much more than a hunt for meat. It was a hunt for my own inner connectedness to the earth, and an affirmation of the renewal of the life force, through active participation in the cycle of life and death. Hunting grounded me and humbled me, bringing me closer to my creator and my own mortality. It served as a reminder. Life is so fragile. Death is so final. Time is so short. This is not a dress rehearsal — live now!

I always went alone even though I had friends who offered, even begged, to come with me. I always (tactfully) turned them down. Somehow I knew that I needed this time by myself, for myself. My hunt was not a social event. It was more of a vision quest, an annual rite of passage, the acknowledgment of the ending of another year, and the ticking of my personal time clock, all rolled into one. My hunt was a time of quiet reflection and a search for new direction.

I had used the same campsite for three or maybe four years. Like the surrounding country, it had taken on a comfortable familiarity that added ritualistic symbolism to my annual enterprise. Because I knew there would still be plenty of good grass left in the high mountain meadows that bordered my camp, on this particular occasion I decided to bring two horses: a riding horse and a packhorse.

In past years I had ridden in with my camping gear on my riding horse. After I had shot my elk, I walked out with a load of meat tied to my saddle. It usually took three or four tedious trips, walking out and riding back in, to get the entire job done. Each round trip took a day. The addition of a packhorse would cut down on the number of trips needed to pack out the elk and retrieve my camping gear. Besides that, because I usually hunted close to camp and left my horse tied out in my absence, I figured a buddy would help keep both horses occupied and happy.

I was riding my Peruvian Paso stallion Carmel. He was a veteran of many backcountry forays, and I knew I could depend on him to be the sensible gentleman I had come to know and appreciate. My packhorse was a lesser-known entity, an Appaloosa filly named Mighty Sadie, just three years old and graduating from her first season under saddle. I had already tried the packsaddle out on her in the comparative safety of my ranch arena. She had shown no signs of trauma or negative reaction. In fact, she behaved fine. I was looking forward to getting a little extra work on her, out on the trail before winter brought an end to the year's training.

Everything had gone like clockwork. Riding into camp, the weather was warm and pleasant. The few remaining leaves that still decorated the trees gave a spark of color to an otherwise sepia-toned scene. Carmel and Sadie seemed to be hitting it off great. He talked sweetly to her under his breath, and she seemed to be impressed and reassured. She followed along easily, making my job with the lead rope a piece of cake.

Once we got to our campsite, I turned them both out after belling and hobbling them, just in case they decided to get frisky. No problem! They were both too busy chowing down on the good grass to pay much attention to each other. Their two small figures, dwarfed by the peaks that surrounded them, made a tranquil pastoral scene. I felt at peace with the world.

By the time I got my tent set up and cooked my evening meal, it was already getting dark. Night falls quickly in the short days of late fall. It can take you by surprise if you aren't paying attention. But I was alert, turned on, and tuned in to my mountain environment, probably the result of being all alone and aware of my solitude and vulnerability.

It's important not to tie horses to anything too light. If they can drag it easily, they may think it's chasing them. If a horse is frightened in this way, you can have a real runaway on your hands, and your horse could end up seriously hurt in the process. Make sure, therefore, that you tie your horse to something sturdy and solid.

I heard the clatter of hooves on the slide rock, far above me, right at timberline. The sound brought a smile to my face and a surge of excitement that hit me like a fist, right in the chest.

By the time the last rays of light were receding into the west, I had tied my horses to their individual high lines and was indulging in my last cup of coffee. A couple of Fig Newton cookies topped off my repast. I turned in early and fell asleep almost immediately. A couple of times during the night I crawled out of my warm cocoon to check on the night sky and visit the horses. A quick inspection assured me that all was well and I returned to my dreams.

Next morning, well before first light, I was up, warming myself on the outside with my little gas stove (brought into the vestibule of my tent) and on the inside with a bowl of hot oat-

meal and a steaming cup of fresh-brewed coffee. In the dark, I gave a last check to the horses. They were fine. So was I. I was ready to go hunting!

Just as I was about to throw out the last dregs of my coffee, I heard the clatter of hooves on the slide rock, far above me, right at timberline. The sound brought a smile to my face and a surge of excitement that hit me like a fist, right in the chest.

I strained to hear every minute sound in the crisp, cold early morning air. Yes, there was no doubt about it! A herd of elk was moving from left to right across the talus slope that wrapped itself around the flank of the mountain, with its main ridge directly above my camp. I strained to see, but nothing appeared. It was still too dark. Still, I knew they were there, moving lazily along, taking their time, probably about five hundred yards or so off my left shoulder.

I decided my best bet was to make a big swing out and around to my right, then climb a narrow avalanche chute that led up to timberline. That path promised easier access to the elk's elevation. Young aspens found a foothold in the shallow soil, stabilizing the loose scree that covered most of the mountainside. Twisted and disfigured, they held on in spite of being bent over, winter after winter, by the downward creep and flow of the snow pack. I had no trouble moving quickly up through the meadow.

Soon I was in the trees, gaining more and more altitude as the angle of my path became steeper. Huge chunks of rock took the place of handhold-sized vegetation. Finally, as I was about to run out of trees, my path and an obvious elk trail crossed each other. I figured it was high enough. I settled myself into a clump of little saplings where I could hide, wait, and watch.

Time went by. Nothing happened. Then all of a sudden all hell broke loose below me. Bang, bang, bang, bang! It sounded as if a war had just broken out, and in my neighborhood, too! Hunters, coming along the main trail down near my camp, had seen (or heard) the elk and opened fire on them. I couldn't believe it! They had to be over a half-mile away.

The elk started running. At first I couldn't see them, but I sure could hear them. They were close and coming right toward me. I could see the hunters, though — little specks of blaze orange, moving around excitedly down in an opening almost surrounded by aspen trees. They kept shooting. The elk were getting closer. So were the shots. I could actually hear the whine followed by a hollow thud as the lead struck nearby.

ELK WERE NOW STREAMING BY ME, splitting into two groups, one going above me, the other below me. They were so panicked that they paid me hardly any attention. And as they ran, the hunters kept right on shooting.

It all happened so fast. I was too angry to be scared. I didn't know whether to jump up or keep still. Like ghosts, the elk were gone. I could see the hunters looking with field glasses to see if they had hit anything. I knew they had, because some of the elk were limping and one was blowing blood bubbles, a sure sign that it had been shot in the lungs.

What the hunters saw, however, was me, giving them the universal sign of my evaluation of their unsportsman-like conduct. They moved out of the clearing, into the woods, and were gone. They didn't even come up to see if they had killed or wounded anything. I never saw them again.

Then I heard an elk puffing, coming slowly along the trail. It was a spike bull, a young male with new antlers. He was obviously shot and seemed confused, sad, and helpless. When he was almost on top of me, he saw me. He just stood there, his head dropped, resigned and waiting. I slowly raised my rifle, took aim, and squeezed. My bullet ended his life instantly, mercifully, and with respect. Even though he was already wounded, he died with dignity. I was relieved and deeply saddened. I wept.

I sat quietly with him and waited for the life to leave his body. I told him that we were brothers. Wherever he was going, I too would soon be following. Life is short, shorter for some than for others. My respect for this young bull elk was offset by my loathing and disgust for the humans who had shot at him, trivializing his life and risking mine, in the name of sport.

By the time I had skinned, dressed, and quartered the elk and carried him (in pieces) down to a place I thought I could bring the horses up into, it was already early afternoon. I figured if I hurried, I could pack out half of the meat, sleep at home that night, and come back the following morning for the other half. I hustled back to camp, saddled Carmel, and put the packsaddle on Sadie. Then I headed up into the trees to where I had stashed the kill.

As we drew close, the horses must have smelled the dead elk. They started to snort and blow. Carmel was willing (though reluctantly) to do as I asked, but Sadie would have no part of it. She was ready to bolt and head straight for home, unloaded. I tried everything in the book, but I couldn't get her anywhere near that elk. She was in a lather and, frankly, so was I. But it did neither of us any good. She was not going to budge. She convinced me that she'd rather die than go a step farther.

It was all I could do to keep her under control, stay in the saddle, and not lose hold of Carmel's lead rope.

I tried a new strategy. I tied her to a tree, brought the elk quarters to her, and tried to pack her there. She, in turn, tried to kill me. Finally, being afraid someone (me) would get really hurt, I gave up.

I unsaddled both horses, switched saddles, and packed half the elk and the skinned hide and horns on good old Carmel. Then, after rechecking my cinch, I mounted Sadie. After much resistance on her part, and physical and verbal persuasion on my part, I finally got hold of Carmel's lead rope. Because Sadie wanted to run and buck, I doubled her and pulled her around in small circles, some to the right, some to the left, with Carmel spinning like a top, trying to keep up. Finally, after a few encores and repeat performances, when I was convinced she wasn't feeling so feisty, we started down the trail: three unhappy, but resigned, campers.

By now the filly was really freaked out. The sight of Carmel, packed with a huge lump of stuff on his back, topped off by the horns, was more than she could handle. The pungent smell of fresh-killed meat made matters even worse. She blew and snorted with every nose full. Her tactics and nervousness were almost more than I could handle as she oscillated unpredictably between fight and flight — neither one a pretty prospect on this steep, rocky trail. It was all I could do to keep her semi-under control, stay in the saddle, and not lose hold of Carmel's lead rope. I felt I needed another hand (or maybe two)! I wished I were headed uphill, to take a little more starch out of this horse. Instead, we had to go almost straight down.

Somehow I finally managed to get going without getting myself thrown off. Little by little the filly settled down to the work at hand, keeping her feet under herself and paying attention to the trail instead of the big bad bogeyman that she was afraid was going to eat her from behind. I, too, started to relax, feeling that the worst was over and I would probably survive this expedition after all. And besides, at least the weather was holding up! I took a couple of deep breaths. It was, in fact, a beautiful, sunshiny day. Thank God for small favors.

I had tied a knot in the end of Carmel's lead rope so that it wouldn't slip out of my gloved hand and get away from me.

From time to time the filly wanted to prance and dance, lunging forward, leaving the deliberately moving stallion behind. This left me stretched out, leaning back over my saddle, trying to hold on and not be pulled in half; holding back one, even as I encouraged the other.

After we had successfully managed a few more miles, I thought things had settled down enough for me to stop and check Carmel's load. After all, he had been bearing the brunt of this evacuation. The heavy hindquarters of the elk, swinging from side to side with each downhill step, put great pressure on his shoulders as he tried to keep the weight from getting out of control. I was afraid that if the saddle slid any farther forward, it would topple him over on his face. He was a little horse, not much over fourteen hands. He made up in heart what he lacked in size. Even so, I felt I owed it to him to give him a break from time to time. He deserved it!

At one point, the trail went up and over a little saddle and then ran between two small hills that were covered with giant aspens. For a short stretch, about the length of football field, it

was fairly flat, a perfect place to rest and readjust the load. I stepped down from Sadie's back, untied and dropped her lead rope to the ground, and wrapped the knotted end of Carmel's rope around the front of my saddle. I didn't tie her up. That turned out to be a major mistake.

As I moved back to check on Carmel, the filly came unglued. Without warning, she bolted forward. Somehow Carmel's lead rope got wedged under her saddle. Before I could do anything, she was dragging him at full gallop, heading straight down the trail. I just stood there for a moment, helplessly watching the incredible, horrible scene.

Poor little Carmel was jerked forward, his head held out poker straight. Every few steps, the filly would kick at him in midflight. He'd dodge her hooves as best he could, even as he was dragged unceremoniously down the trail. The elk, of course, was flying all over the place, frightening the filly even more. Like a runaway train, it didn't look as if they could be stopped before they destroyed their cargo and themselves.

The trail we were on switchbacked around and down the hill, coming back in our direction, below us. In desperation I practically threw myself over the edge, sliding, crashing, and bounding downhill, hoping to stop the horses as they came by on the trail below. Somehow, I made it! The filly saw me standing there, waving my arms. She ran around in a half-circle and headed back up the trail. She was still dragging Carmel and still kicking wildly at him.

I gave chase. After running back past our starting point (where we had originally stopped), she ran off the trail up a little draw and tangled her lead rope in some fallen aspen trees. Both horses stood there, sides heaving, lungs blowing and panting, coats covered in sweat, exhausted. Carmel had blood coming out of a few places where she had nailed him. One blow had caught him right in the teeth, but he seemed no worse for wear.

As we all calmed down and cooled off, I unloaded Carmel and repacked him from scratch. As I said, he was a trooper! He put up with this attack on his dignity and did it with style. This time, I tied up the filly!

Soon we were back on the trail, making good progress. I could see the trail far below where it came out of the aspens and crossed some big open talus slopes, a sea of giant dinner-plate-shaped rocks. They were all stacked on edge, covering a huge section of the mountainside. Even with this well-worn trail running through them, they clattered and banged underfoot as we picked our way carefully through them. We managed this obstacle with

Packing up the last few items, I'm ready to hit the trail once more.

no trouble, then climbed a small hill, came through a low drift fence, and crested a little bush-covered knoll.

I HAD JUST PULLED UP for a moment to survey the surrounding mountains and let the horses catch their breath before we tackled the last long downhill stretch. All of a sudden, four little mules jumped up, out of nowhere, as if they were tiny trolls that had been shot up out of the ground. This was more than Sadie could bear. She reared up, went right over backward, and landed flat on her back in the rocks, totally forgetting about me, my saddle, Carmel, or the elk.

I was caught totally off guard. I managed to jump off as she was coming over. Even so, my foot caught in the rocks, and before I could scramble away she had fallen on top of me, pinning my leg. I heard a crunching sound, like a dry twig breaking. For a split second I thought, She's broken my leg, and now she's going to roll over on me and crush me, too. With my free leg, I pushed her off her back in the other direction. A moment later she was back on her feet, staring bug-eyed at the mules, who were tied to four trees. I lay on the ground, checking myself out, wondering why I didn't feel any (serious) pain.

Then it dawned on me. The cracking noise wasn't my leg! It was my rifle. I pulled myself to my feet, dusted myself off, and pulled my rifle out of its scabbard. Sure enough, the stock was cracked and there was a brand-new ding in the barrel.

I felt heartsick. You see, this rifle was special to me. I had lovingly customized its stock, hand-rubbed linseed oil into its satiny smooth finish, and cut a pistol grip cap of elk horn from the first elk I ever shot to personalize its appearance. I had carried it for years and years. Every elk and deer that I had ever killed, I had shot with this rifle. Every animal I had shot at, I had killed cleanly. Somehow, I felt a deep sadness, as though I had lost a very close friend. Only time, and a shooting session at the rifle range, would confirm my deepest fears about the seriousness of this incident. But right at that moment, somehow I knew that some chapter in my life had come to a close.

Sadie stood still, letting me mount with ease as though nothing had happened. Carmel came willingly along behind, carrying his load without complaint. The four little mules moved around their trees, watching us go off down the trail. Everything seemed so easy; it was almost as though nothing unusual had ever happened. Only the scars on the rifle stock and blue barrel bore witness to the traumatic event.

In an hour we had negotiated the steepest sections of trail and were cruising along the relatively flat terrain at the upper end of the valley, bound for the trailhead. There was a big hunting camp located in an aspen meadow, right where the trail crossed the stream. As we rode by, some hunters, hanging around their fire and drinking beer, called out to me, "Hey, did ya see some little mules tied up to trees up on a hill a mile or so up the trail?"

A lot of ignoble thoughts went racing through my mind. I admit it. I was tempted to share those thoughts with them, but seeing the party mood they were in (with the help of the beer), I thought better of it. Instead, I just nodded, tipped my hat, and said, "Yeah, I saw them." Without exchanging another word, I rode on.

Sometimes, when you have a chance to reflect on an incident or a period in your life, you sense that you were being sent a message. Change is inevitable, an undeniable feature of life. Usually it's not noticeable or punctuated dramatically enough for us to be consciously aware of it. But some things are final. You don't need to be told. You just know it. I have never been hunting since, and I doubt that I will ever go again. I guess it's fair to say that I got the message!

Just Another Perfect Day

It was turning out to be just another perfect day, one in a series of similar backcountry horseback trips. Late summer in the high Colorado Rockies is usually warm and dry — and perfect for comfortable camping and long lazy days of easy riding, interrupted only by quiet interludes of laid-back relaxing. As we climbed into the high country, we left the heat of the desert and the tension of our high-strung, humdrum lives behind. Stress melts away quickly as the tempo of the mountains take over. It was wonderful to feel so content, so present in the moment, and to be enjoying such good company.

My friend Jim had been after me for months to take him on a horse camping trip. Finally, I had found a few open days in my schedule. We had made the commitment to just do it, and now, here we were. It was great to be alive. Even though he wasn't saying much, the big grin spread all over Jim's face told me that he was feeling the same way.

We were riding through the West Elks, one of my very favorite places. The mountains aren't high enough to attract the attention of the hordes of hikers and climbers who congregate around the fourteeners (Colorado's 14,000-foot peaks). Still this wilderness area has a special, rugged topography that gives it a feeling of remoteness and isolation, a quality of solitude that is hard to find these days. You rarely run into anyone else on the trail. In fact, one time I went for eight days alone, without ever seeing another soul.

On this trip I was riding my little Peruvian Paso stallion Carmel, as I had done many times before. Jim was riding a broom-tailed, leopard Appaloosa gelding named Rocky. And just for the heck of it, I had brought along a little bay Peruvian mare named Alba. This was really an afterthought. We hadn't intended to bring a packhorse. Normally we travel light, camping low-impact style and carrying all our gear on our riding horses. But Alba was in heat and was being bred by Carmel. Even though it was a little late in the season I wanted to make sure she got pregnant rather than wait another entire year. We had already bred her once, and I needed to let Carmel continue to cover her at least every other day until she went out of heat. What choice did I have? I decided to bring her along.

Even though she was only four years old and had gone under saddle (lightly) only the previous year, Alba was a gentle soul and took easily to her new task. Besides, our equipment was light; her entire load couldn't have been more than fifty pounds. She didn't even seem to notice it when we loaded the panniers

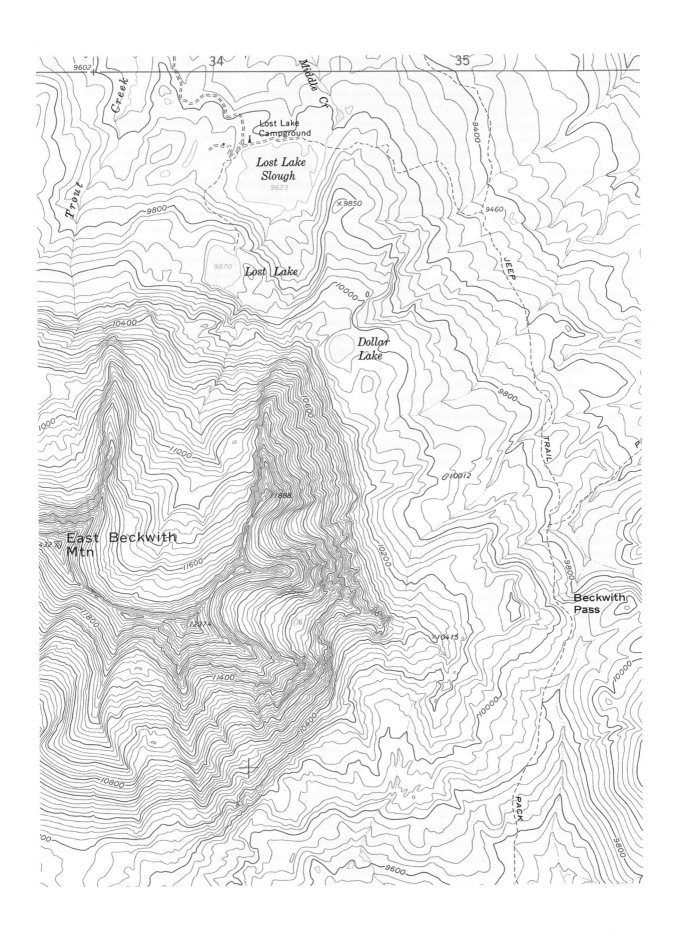

The air was still and cool. As we tucked in the horses and prepared for bed, we were already looking forward to another glorious day.

onto her packsaddle. She was mostly interested in Carmel. In fact, I didn't even need to lead her. I just tied her lead rope around her neck (with a bowline), turned her loose, and let her come along on her own. Wherever Carmel went, Alba would follow. Jim agreed with me when I said, "This is great!" Carmel, obviously, felt the same. Of the four of us males (Jim, Carmel, Rocky, and me), Carmel was the only one who was going to enjoy the company of a *femme fatale* on this expedition.

DAYS AND NIGHTS quickly melted into each other, taking on the warm fuzzy feelings of a Japanese watercolor or a satisfying dream. The second night out we camped near a little lake, well off in the meadow, of course, along a nice stand of bordering aspen trees. It was a beautiful camp, well protected from the west wind, and offered a glorious view of the tallest mountain peaks off to the east.

The horses thought they were in heaven, too. The grass in the meadow was up at full height, offering a bountiful banquet to the hardy appetites of Carmel, Alba, and Rocky. After stuffing ourselves on a mulligan stew, washed down with plenty of coffee and topped off with biscuits, margarine, and honey, Jim and I settled down to enjoy the grand finale: a blazing sunset, followed by the soft pink shades of alpenglow slowly retreating from the peaks and disappearing into the blackness of a high altitude night. The air was still and cool. As we tucked in the horses and prepared for bed, we were already looking forward to another glorious day.

Now, I'll admit it, Jim and I were becoming down right derelict. We stayed in our sleeping bags until the sun popped over the skyline ridge and warmed us in our tent. We waited until we were almost driven out by the heat. Of course, I stuck my head out from time to time, just to relieve my guilty conscience and assure myself that the horses were getting along okay. And, of course, they were. I had brewed up a pot of coffee, and Jim and I were just lying there, half in/half out of our bags, tent flap thrown back, admiring the horses and soaking in the scenery.

I have to tell you, Carmel was an exceptionally beautiful horse. Everywhere we went, people came up to see him and admire him. He was the color of a new copper penny, with a flaxen mane and tail. Like many Peruvian Pasos, his mane and forelock were very long and wavy, a characteristic he inherited from his Andalusian ancestry. He was a proud horse and held his head high. In fact, his forelock was so long, it came down and covered his eyes. It was so thick, you sometimes had to wonder how he could see where he was going. He wasn't very big, but he was truly magnificent.

I was fully immersed in this pleasant reverie when I heard the sound of horses' hooves coming right toward us. Carmel, Rocky, and Alba heard them, too, and got very excited. Sure enough, four cowboys, all decked out in the finest buckaroo regalia, came riding straight into our camp. They all wore those big old-timey ten-gallon hats, with silk wild rags tied around their necks. Wide suspenders held up their jeans. High-topped, high-heeled cowboy boots and fancy fringed chinks completed the outfits. They wore large, fancy *vaquero* spurs with big rowels and jingle bobs, too, and they all were chewing tobacco. Of course, they were riding big ol' quarter horses: really big horses with big bones and big muscles; horses built to do the hard work of real cowboys; the pickup trucks of horses; strong, Spartan, and utilitarian. These guys looked like they rode right off a movie set or the cover of a glossy Western magazine.

The cowboys rode right up to our tent in a kind of aggressive, threatening manner. It was obvious: Even though we were camped on public land, they thought we were trespassers on their turf. They sat there, looking down on us, as we lay there sipping our coffee. It's a known fact that cowboys always get up early. It's part of their mystique. You see, I know, because some years earlier I had been a cowboy myself. Not only did I have the cowboy outfit but I even had the job to go with it, pushing hundreds of cow-calf units around the mountains near Crested Butte, Colorado.

The best trails are the ones that lead you to yourself.

Well, as I said, these cowboys looked down on us with contempt and disgust. The sun was up and we were still in bed! They looked at our camping gear with disgust, too — obviously the type of sissy stuff you'd expect some hippie environmentalist to use. And, finally, they looked at our horses with disgust: couldn't chase a cow on those funny lookin' little horses to save your *sombrero!* They didn't have to say anything. You could read their rancor all over their faces.

Nonchalantly, I crawled out of the tent and stood there in front of them, wearing nothing but my jockey shorts. That seemed to turn their hard gaze away. I could tell they felt a little awkward, staring at me, dressed (or undressed) as I was. I said, "Why don't you gentlemen step down and join us for a fresh brewed cappuccino?" After they finished chewin' and spittin', they brusquely turned down my offer. After all, they had cows to chase, serious business to attend to, and were not just out for a pleasant ride. I said, "Well, drop in again sometime, boys." They said, "Much obliged."

Just as they were about to go, I noticed that one of them was really eyeballing Carmel. He had a very serious look on his face. I could see he was really working something over in his mind. After considerable cogitation, he leaned out away from his horse and spit again. Finally, he turned to me and asked, "Do you curl that animal's hair?" I answered, "Sure do, first thing every mornin'. Why d'ya think we ain't broke camp and hit the trail yet?" That was, apparently, more than they could stand. Like desperadoes looking for the OK Corral, they spurred their cold-blooded cayuses and rode off in a cloud of dust. Once again, we were alone.

By midafternoon, we had negotiated the rougher stretches of the trail, and were enjoying the good life as we rode the last few miles to the road head. The trail had widened out enough for us to ride side by side, with Alba following along behind Carmel. I don't know how long we had been going on like that, just gabbin' and gawkin', when suddenly I realized that I didn't hear Alba's footsteps behind us. I looked around. Sure enough, she was gone!

Immediately, we turned around and started to backtrack up the trail. We went on and on, but no sight of Alba. How could we have come so far and not even noticed she was missing? I was getting really concerned, but I kept my cool, not wanting to blow my macho image in front of my sidekick. Later, he admitted that he was pretty rattled by the thoughts of losing her, too. Then, as we rounded a bend in small switchback that wound around the hill, making an easy incline up to the next bench, we saw her. Well, at least we saw her feet, that is. She was below us, off the side of the trail with all four legs sticking straight up in midair. They waved gently, like bulrushes in the breeze. In fact, she seemed quite calm, as though she was just waiting for us to come rescue her. Somehow, she'd fallen off the trail, rolled upside down, and pinned the packsaddle between two rocks, which were holding her securely in place. We undid the cinches of the packsaddle (upside-down, of course) and rolled her off her pedestal. She shook herself off like a wet dog but seemed no worse for wear. We repacked her and were back on the trail in no time. She whinnied a hello to Carmel and, like a true lady, acted as though nothing had happened.

Memories and Rewards

For me, the less remarkable memories of my many back-country horse trips are the ones that have subtly seeped into my subconscious and filled me with a sense of satisfaction and fulfilment. I know that only by doing do we truly come to know. Experience is still the best teacher for those who are ready to learn. Like the bear that went over the mountain, the new perspective is the real reward. Life is just a trail, and the best trails are the ones that lead you to yourself.

Life Is a Trail

Life is a trail
towards a
lone mountaintop
it's a track
through the desert
the wind blows away

So live for
adventure
live wild and free
there's no place
to get to
your quest is
"to be"

And keep
on the move
to stay strong
and alive
count each day
a success
if you can say
"I survived"

— Don West

UNSADDLING AT THE END OF THE TRAIL

There is a proper sequence to follow while tacking and untacking your horse. Doing things out of order can cause a catastrophe. So make this your habit when unsaddling: First undo the crupper, then the breast collar, and lastly the cinch.

1. First I remove my pommel bag.

2. Then I untie and remove the cantle bag and the saddlebags.

3. Be sure to undo the shock-cord stays that attach with Velcro to the girth.

4. Then I remove the bosal. I have designed a bridle system that allows me to remove the bosal without taking off the halter. Another option is to leave the halter on under your bridle.

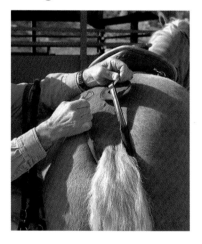

5. Next I undo the crupper and detach it from the saddle.

6. I then undo and remove the breast collar.

The less your horse is without a halter on, the better. There is always a chance he might spook at the very moment you are trying to put the halter on.

7. Finally, I undo the girth.

8. . . . and gently slide the saddle off.

9. Back at the ranch, we hose off the horses to remove the trail dirt and sweat.

I prefer to put the head-gear on last and take it off first (except for the halter, which goes on first and comes off last, of course), but that's just personal preference.

The horses tuck in to a well-deserved dinner.

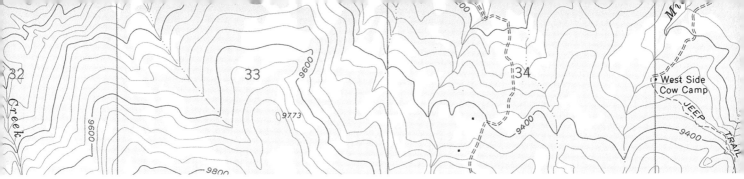

CHAPTER FIVE

Past and Future

CHANGING TIMES FOR TRAIL RIDERS

ver the years my friend Mike Ecker, a trainer of Paso Fino horses, and I have often talked about taking a low-impact backcountry riding-camping trip together. Last summer we decided to stop dreaming about it and just do it!

Mike lives over near Telluride, Colorado, on a huge, high, open mesa. I had taught backpacking and mountaineering in that part of the San Juan Mountains twenty-plus years ago for the Colorado Outward Bound School. From the front porch of Mike's beautiful log home you can see the jagged skyline ridges of Mount Wilson and Wilson Peak. I used to guide students to the top of these two awesome 14,000-foot peaks as part of their Outward Bound course experience. One afternoon, soaking in the warm sun, I said to Mike, "Why not go explore that high country, perhaps doing a traverse around the peak?" And so a plan was hatched, a date was set, and the stage was set for a mini-adventure.

The night before we left, Mike and I went over our maps, selected a tentative route, and located a starting place where we would hit the trail. The maps were U.S. Geological Survey Topographical maps, made around 1960. No matter, the topography doesn't change in thirty years, right? Or so we thought.

Above and opposite: Pack along a small
disposable camera so that you can
record special moments in snapshots.

Next morning we ate a quick breakfast, loaded our two Paso geldings in my trusty old trailer, and headed out to the starting place, only a few miles from Mike's house. We parked the trailer and scouted out the access trail. Sure enough, there it was, just as it was shown on the map; only, much to my surprise, it didn't seem to be used much. Oh well, no matter, we were saddled, packed, and ready to go in no time. Let the adventure begin!

We hadn't gone more than a quarter-mile up the trail when we came to our first major obstacle, a bunch of huge old dead aspen trees blown down over the path. We were on a very steep hillside, so getting up, over, and around each one of these trees was a real challenge. Once past this obstacle we thought we'd have clear sailing, but no such luck. The trail continued to deteriorate until it was hardly more than a deer path, finally breaking off in various directions, leaving us forced to make a difficult decision: Should we go on, using map, compass, and dead reckoning, or turn back? Thinking about having to recross the downed aspen, we chose bushwhacking.

All of a sudden, in the middle of nowhere, we came to a sign that read: "Private Property — Keep Out!" How could that be? We were in the wilderness! But no, apparently this land was a posted private preserve, even though it was presently positively primitive. We figured, what the heck, we've come too far now to turn back, and the public land must start just up ahead, so let's go for it. After all, we're not hurting anything, and besides, who'd object to two ol' lost cowboys just riding on through?

We crashed and thrashed through the aspen forest for a few more miserable miles. Then we heard the sound of a bulldozer coming from somewhere up ahead. It didn't seem possible, but by golly, there it was! Figuring it was better to find whoever it was than to be found, we rode over to ask the equipment operator where we were. He told us we were on some former ranchland that had been sold off for recreational home development. He was putting in ponds for the new 40-acre home sites.

Farther up the way we hit a gravel road, one that wasn't on our map. To shorten our stay on private property, we decided to head up it. Soon a Suburban came flying by. The driver slammed on the brakes, backed up, and read us the riot act. He was the caretaker, and we were in danger of being arrested for trespassing.

Now this was marked on our map as an access trail leading onto Forest Service-administered land. In years past the original ranchers and sheepherders who owned these huge homesteads didn't mind having a few harmless riders pass by on the trail; in fact, they were probably happy for the company. But now things are different. We were criminals, lawbreakers, no better than thieves, rapists, or murderers. Well, after we explained our misplaced presence, the caretaker agreed to let us ride up to his place. He'd show us a shortcut to our trail up the mountain. Horses do help you make friends, even under less than civil circumstances.

As we rode farther up the ridge road toward his place and started to break out of the aspen, we could see the land falling away all around us. We could also see the spider web of new roads invading what had until recently been unspoiled land as far as the eye could see. These private roads all led to multi-million-dollar trophy homes, recently built or just being built on every hilltop or "perfect spot." Yes, the ultra-wealthy have taken over the Colorado high country ranchland, right up to the Forest Service or Park Service borders.

We finally arrived at a huge home where our new host met us to give us our directions. I commented on what a big place he had. Oh no, this was just the "gatehouse." The "main lodge" was farther up the road. Wow! And, believe me, these city folk aren't interested in sharing this beautiful open space with their fellowman. No sir, their goal is to have their own fenced-in private paradise, replete with all the amenities of city civilization. Many of these wilderness palaces now have their own helipads, so the absentee owners can buzz in for the occasional weekend without having to waste driving time.

Lighting began to flash on the peaks above us. The sky turned black and evil, as dark as night.

By the time Mike and I crossed over onto public property it was already late afternoon. Checking the map and finding our location, we could see that the stream running through the open meadow in front of us was probably our last chance for a reasonable, relatively flat campsite. The flank of the mountain loomed up just ahead of us. Once we started up there, there would be no easy campsite and no feed for our horses. After discussing our alternatives, we opted to call it a day.

Sitting around camp, sipping cups of freshly brewed coffee, and admiring our Paso horses as they contentedly grazed the meadow bunchgrass, we reflected on the trials and tribulations of the day's journey. What we had seen wasn't unique to this area. The urban invasion is happening all over the backcountry. Everywhere you go more and more people want to use less and less land. The pressures for prioritizing land use and making choices about who can do what will only intensify as time goes by. It is a sad reality. For me, wilderness is synonymous with freedom, and every day there is less and less of both. I'm glad I lived where I did, when I did, while there were still wild places to explore, unfettered and unrestricted.

The next day Mike and I headed up the switchback trail into the high alpine country above timberline. We soon found ourselves making a long traverse on a razor-thin trail with a thousand-foot drop-off on one side and a cliff wall rising above our heads on the other. As the afternoon approached, the weather deteriorated rapidly and the temperature dropped. The wind blew fiercely, driving rain and sleet hard into our faces. Lighting began to flash on the peaks above us. The sky turned black and evil, as dark as night. The horses began to get nervous, slipping and sliding on the now muddy trail. You could smell ozone in the air. Our hair began to stand on end from static electricity. Another adventure was underway.

No matter what transpires in our human world down below, the mountains have their own laws that are much larger and more implacable than ours. By tuning in to these greater truths, by living our lives in harmony with nature's own rules, we ensure protection of our precious wilderness areas and of our own true selves. 🐎

USING AND ABUSING PUBLIC LAND

Many ranchers have had grazing permits (at below market value) on public lands for so long that they've come to think of them as their own personal property. They view all other users as trespassers.What's more, they have a powerful lobby to back them up.

The fact is, it's been a common practice to run more than the allotted number of cows on these permitted government lands almost from day one. Often, cows are run in "pools." Ranchers get together, mix their cattle, and have an association rider move the herd around, keeping them on good grass and water. It's not uncommon for these herds to number in the many hundreds. As you can imagine, this makes it pretty tough to know what's going on out there. The bottom line is that the government administers a system that spends the taxpayer's money on what amounts to nothing more than a rancher's subsidy.

At the same time, the federal agencies are so underfunded and understaffed that they hardly ever get out in the field to check up on things. It's easy to get away with overruns and abuses and never get caught. And, if someone gets caught, the worst they'll get is a slap on the hand. In fact, there seems to be a growing sympathy for ranchers, probably due to the renewed national nostalgia for simpler times. Everybody who runs cattle on public land knows this (and takes advantage of it).

And therefore, they do things pretty much as they please. Without interference, this has become an accepted and expected way of life. In fact, in my thirty years of riding the backcountry, cowboying, packing, guiding, and camping, I've never once run into a ranger.

The end result? Our federal land, especially wilderness, takes a hell of a beating from the cattle: Grass gets munched down to bare ground in large areas, waterholes are turned into ugly mud puddles, riparian areas get trampled and spoiled, and slimy cow pies appear everywhere, especially under every decent-sized tree, which is usually right where I want to put my tent. Most of the time, no one is watching these cows. They go wherever they want until they've eaten up everything in the area and it's necessary to move them to a new location.

It's been a way of life for so long that most people don't even think about it or question it. But, it does set the stage for conflict and animosity between cowboys and environmentalists.

From my point of view, things are a little out of kilter. Try to picture a few hundred cows in your favorite wilderness drainage area. Now, multiply that bunch of cows times the drainages all across the country. Try to imagine the amount of damage done by all those cows to our public lands. A lot of times it's hard to find anything left for your horse to eat after the cows have been through. Then, try to mentally match that to the impact of four horses, ridden by people who are concerned about the environment and are trying to do everything possible to leave no trace of their passage. How does their impact compare?

BACKCOUNTRY STEWARDS

The United States Forest Service and other government agencies that supervise public land are starting to feel and respond to pressure from other environmentally conscious groups of backcountry users. They are trying to educate the horse-packing community by putting out flyers that encourage better low-impact practices. I applaud them for that!

Still, it's up to all of us horse users to work together to improve our horse-packing and camping techniques and get in step with other backcountry users. If we are going to preserve our rights to ride the federal lands, we need to project a responsible, environmentally friendly image. We need to encourage low-impact horse camping and show that we can be good stewards of the backcountry we love to ride and camp in.

Of course, we can do it. The real question is, *Will we*

do it? Or will it just be another case of too little, too late?

A Parting Shot

We live in a world filled with overwhelming problems. Everywhere you look there seems to be something going on, often on a colossal scale.

The natural resources of the earth are being depleted at an ever-escalating pace. The tropical rain forests, which hold the genetic keys to biological diversity and maintain the earth's oxygen/carbon dioxide balance, are being systematically destroyed right in front of our eyes. In thirty years, they and all the life-forms they nurture and sustain will be gone. Every day, alarming numbers of irreplaceable species become extinct — gone forever.

A Delicate Dance

Throughout our history, we humans, with our insatiable curiosity and our never-ending appetite for answers, have created numerous mythologies that attempt to explain our presence on this little speck in the universe we call Planet Earth. Most of these myths seem amusing and quaint to us modern, sophisticated, city-bound people. "Primitive" cultures, however, recognized their own direct dependence on the natural world and understood themselves to be part of, not separate from, the environment that surrounded them. Their religions and traditions were built on and reflected the common bond and inner dependency of all living things. It was the delicate dance that sustained their very existence. Their creation stories expressed their inner dependency, their deep humility, and their sense of reverence for all life.

In modern times, our self-imposed isolation from the roots of our existence has left us feeling empty and alien. The current popularly held mythology of the Western world views man as separate from all other life-forms on this planet. We see ourselves as the chosen ones. Our mass communication capabilities and the

almost complete annihilation of less aggressive societal groups by our dominant culture have made it even more difficult for us to see ourselves as we really are.

The View from Space

Let's step outside ourselves for a moment. How would we appear to alien, extraterrestrial eyes? From outer space the earth could be viewed as a complex living organism, a single entity with all the plants and animals comprising the various organs and tissues necessary for its existence. Given that view, people would be seen as just one of many life forms. We would most likely be classified as a cancer, a malignant growth that, although insignificant in small numbers, has rapidly multiplied and spread itself throughout the body of Mother Earth.

Instead of being the masters of our own destiny, we are probably going to become the victims of our own built-in biological fate. As we all know, cancer eventually kills the host organism, thus destroying itself.

Is that what's happening to us? Of course, only time will tell. But time no longer seems to be on our side. In fact, our time seems to be running out.

What can we do? How do we cope with all this bad news? How do we maintain a balance and give our lives meaning?

What Have We Done

What have we done
To our Mother the Earth
To her lakes
And her streams
And her seas?

What have we done
To the land of our birth
To the birds
And the beasts
And the trees?

What have we done
To the source of our mirth
To the skies
And the air
That we breathe?

What have we done
To attest to our worth
To be sure
We'll live on
When we leave?

— Don West

It's the stones in the path of the water that give the stream its music.

For me, there is only one answer. When I feel the pressures of the world closing in on me, when everything seems futile and empty, I rely on a remedy that works wonders in restoring my physical and mental health, rekindling my spirit, and renewing my understanding of my place in the universe. What do I do? You guessed it. I pack my gear, saddle my horse, and head for the most remote piece of country I can find. My motto is, Have saddle — will travel.

Almost everything I know that's worth knowing I learned in the school of hard knocks. It would please me to think that reading one of my stories might save some fellow traveler from the inconvenience, discomfort, or real danger (for rider or horse) that I experienced to gain this knowledge. At the same time, I have to admit that some of my most difficult and dangerous experiences have been my most rewarding.

Plenty of Lessons to Learn

Fortunately, Mother Nature has a seemingly endless bag of tricks up her sleeve. There'll always be plenty of new lessons to learn. Just remember: It's the stones in the path of the water that give the stream its music. I have found that the mountains speak loudest to those who pay in sweat to hear their voices. Life is not a dress rehearsal. In fact, this may well be the final curtain call.

So don't wait. Go out and live life to the max. May you always ride a good horse, and may you ride him well. And remember, it's a fine line that divides creative from crazy, so have fun, but be careful out there.

Saddle up — let's ride! Happy trails.

One with the Earth

I am one with the Earth
I live on
And the Earth
is one with me
I share a bond
A kinship
With everything I see

Through the joy,
the pain,
and the sorrow
That life on earth
must bring
I walk the path
of brotherhood
With every living thing

As a wandering child
of the Universe
I proclaim my
right to be
A speck of dust
A point of light
A spirit
Wild and free.

— Don West

Index

OTHER STOREY TITLES
YOU WILL ENJOY

101 Arena Exercises by Cherry Hill. A ringside exercise book for riders who want to improve their own and their horses' skills, presented in a unique "read and ride" format. Comb-bound to allow hanging in the barn or lying flat on a barrel for easy reference. 224 pages. Paperback. ISBN 0-88266-316-X.

The Basics of Western Riding by Charlene Strickland. A complete guide to the exciting world of Western riding, including choosing a horse, selecting and fitting tack, training, problem-solving, and competing. 144 pages. Paperback. ISBN 1-58017-030-7.

Horse Handling and Grooming by Cherry Hill. A user-friendly guide, complete with 350 how-to photographs, presenting correct techniques for leading, haltering, tying, grooming, clippng, bathing, braiding, hoof handling, and more. 160 pages. Paperback. ISBN 0-88266-956-7.

Horse Health Care by Cherry Hill. Practical advice, complete with 350 how-to photographs, on dozens of essential skills, including daily examination, restraint, leg wrapping, hoof care, administering shots, dental care, wound care, and more. 160 pages. Paperback. ISBN 0-88266-955-9.

Horsekeeping on a Small Acreage: Facilities Design and Management by Cherry Hill. How to design safe and functional facilities for your horse. 192 pages. Paperback. ISBN 0-88266-596-0.

Riata Ranch Cowboy Girls by Tom Maier and Rebecca Ferran Witter. The thrilling true story of the troupe of teenage trick riders who have taken the world by storm, with their training tips and insights, photographed in full color. 160 pages. Hardcover. ISBN 1-58017-365-9.

Starting & Running Your Own Horse Business by Mary Ashby McDonald. How to run a successful business and make the most of your investments in horses, facilities, and equipment. 160 pages. Paperback. ISBN 0-88266-960-5.

Storey's Guide to Raising Horses by Heather Smith Thomas. The complete reference for the horse owner with detailed coverage of feeding and nutrition, foot care, disease prevention, dental care, breeding, foaling, and caring for the young horse. 512 pages. Paperback. ISBN 1-58017-127-3.

Storey's Horse-Lover's Encyclopedia: An English & Western A-to-Z Guide edited by Deborah Burns. Detailed information on all breeds and disciplines, healthy horse care, tack, terminology, and stable lore, packed with illustrations and charts. 480 pages. Paperback. ISBN 1-58017-336-5.

Trailering Your Horse by Cherry Hill. A photographic guide to low-stress traveling, including selecting a trailer, training, loading, packing, safe driving, and care en route. 160 pages. Paperback. ISBN 1-58017-176-1.

These books and other Storey Books are available at your bookstore, farm store, garden center, or directly from Storey Books, 210 MASS MoCA Way, North Adams, MA 01247, or by calling 1-800-441-5700. Or visit our Web site at www.storey.com.